# Serial Killers

## 6 Horrific Serial Killers' True Crime Stories

### (Six Bloody Fantasies Vol 1)

### Ryan Becker

# Special Thanks

This is a special thanks to the taken time out of their busy schedule to read my work and give me suggestions. Thank you all so much!

Donna

Joan Baker

Gardy Harp

Lisa Millett

Jamie Bothen

Pamela Culp

Jeannie Huie

Evette White

Barbara Davis

Patricia Oliver

James Herington

Linda M Wheeler

Bonnie Kernene

Tonja Marshall

Kathy Morgan

# Table of Contents

# DARK FANTASIES
# TURN REALITY

# Introduction

*"Murderers are not monsters, they're men. And that's the most frightening thing about them."*

- Alice Sebold

In a world of billions of humans, all so naturally different and brought up in distinct cultures, belief systems and communities, it is no surprise that our planet is equally capable of producing the most wonderful heroes and the most disgusting monsters.

We are a curious race, one that seeks day by day to uncover the mysteries of our world and our universe; the only known species that can attest to possessing a consciousness and advanced intelligence. For some, that intelligence is used for seeking answers and finding a way to progress as human beings.

Others, however, allow it to develop into a tool for finding the best way to indulge themselves in pleasure and give free rein to their desires. These are the most dangerous kinds of humans.

The following book is a compilation of the lives of several human beings who gave themselves up to their fantasies — fantasies which were born of violence, murder, and the thirst for blood. Some worked alone, others with accomplices; some were strong and fearless, others used discreet or cowardly methods to kill their victims; some did it because they loved seeing the despair in their victims' faces, others because they believed they were fulfilling an order from higher powers...It matters little, for at the end of the day, they were all murderers of the worst kind.

This collection of stories shall take you across the world and into the minds of very twisted individuals, and it is important you understand that no details shall be left out to protect the sensibilities of our readers; be sure that you shall learn of every terrible act committed by our monsters, as evil as they may have been.

From Robert Pickton — who killed dozens of women and fed them to the pigs on his farm — to Genene Jones — who made children sick in a terribly disturbing attempt at saving them due to her desire to be seen as a 'heroine,' killing many in the process — we are about to embark on a journey, a journey that leads down a bloodstained slope into an abyss of pitch-black darkness.

Be ready, reader, because after you read about these killers...

*...you may not sleep again for a while...*

# ONE

----------------------------

## The Pig Farmer Killer

Canada: the *'Great White North,'* a land of peace and nature. A country which stands with open doors, welcoming those who wish to enter it and better themselves — and the nation — with their work and studies.

It is the home to many wonderful people, but it is, just like any other nation, also not without its rotten apples. **Robert Pickton**, was one such rotten apple.

As such, a misfit was born and raised in the suburban lands of Port Coquitlam, British Columbia; a farmer with little more to care about than his land and the animals within it.

Nevertheless, this simple man would grow up to become a monster that took the lives of dozens of women and felt no remorse at having doing so, as per his confession to a police officer.

Now, let us begin our compilation with the story of *'Pork Chop Rob'*...

## A Simple Farmer

Port Coquitlam is a small, suburban city east of Vancouver, a pleasant place sitting at the confluence of two rivers: the Pitt and the Fraser. Although in recent years its economy has evolved and diversified to include a large amount of industrial and commercial investments, such as metal fabrication, transportation, and high-technology development, it was once a city known for its extensive farmland. Because of its proximity to Vancouver, the farmers in the small city had the right amount of customers to deliver their produce to and were highly successful with their fertile lands, allowing them to leave a substantial inheritance to their heirs.

This was precisely the case with the Pickton's. In 1905, 52 years after the first settlers arrived at the area which would become Port Coquitlam, William Pickton, our killer's great-grandfather, bought a piece of land and began to raise hogs on it. He dedicated his entire life to this business, soon passing it on to his sons and daughters, and their children as well. Leonard Pickton, Robert's father, received an inheritance from William and was able to buy a piece of land near a swamp in 1963, where the killings would take place many years later.

At first, however, Robert and his brother David worked on their land with their parents. A sister, Linda, was raised a city girl in Vancouver, but she was close to her siblings. Robert and David grew up learning everything they needed to know about raising and slaughtering hogs, and soon they became a successful partnership. Incredibly successful in fact. The farmland, purchased for $18,000 in 1963, was valued at $300,000 in 1993. One year later, its value soared to an incredible $7.2 million. The Pickton's had started off with a pig farm and now owned a hog empire.

It didn't take long for others to see viable uses for the Pickton's valuable land, and offers began to arrive: in 1994 and 1995, the Pickton brothers sold three large pieces of the farm for around $1.7, $1.2, and $2.3, totaling $5.16 million. Rob and David weren't just farmers anymore, they were millionaires.

Robert was described as a quiet guy, hard to communicate or start a casual conversation with. He behaved strangely and had a penchant for acting tough, as if he owned the place. A local bartender considered him a weasel and a wannabe despite the rough look he attempted to transmit, and he was believed to be a loner.

Loner or not, Robert and his brother were soon to become celebrities in Port Coquitlam, when they invested part of their fortune in a new property nearby in 1996 and opened a party hall named Piggy's Palace. With their new place and a lot of money at hand, the siblings founded a non-profit charity organization named the "Piggy Palace Good Times Society," which, after receiving permission from the Canadian government itself, aimed to organize, manage, and operate special events, dances, shows, and exhibitions on behalf of service organizations, as well as other groups.

The Palace started off well, with grand, family-friendly costume parties where kids ran around playing and their parents watched as the Pickton's served their very own hogs off a roasting spit, but unnamed visitors noticed how the place began to devolve: prostitutes began to frequent the parties, called in to allow the male visitors some company, while cocaine and other drugs began to flow freely around the party-goers without any attempt to hide it. Mayors were seen at the raves, along with other politicians, business owners, students, and even a large amount of Hells Angels bikers, who enjoyed the chaotic nature of the nights at the Palace.

It wouldn't be long before Robert began to neglect the farming business, his focus solely on the party hall and its activities. He was a millionaire now, and the only uses he had for pigs were fattening them to sell the meat to friends or to the visitors of Piggy's Palace — who got to eat them freshly roasted and with Rob himself cutting the meat off the bones — or to be hauled away to a nearby rendering plant named West Coast Reduction Ltd. The facility was an expansive complex, boasting huge cookers, several administrative buildings, railroad tracks, and massive storage tanks. It continually pumped its products towards the ports for export, and was a walking distance away from Vancouver's most expensive sector, meaning that a great deal of its products ended up in the stores where the wealthy went to buy. What products were produced? Well, anything from bases for commercial products such as lipstick and soap to shampoos and perfumes; all of them made from the unusable remains of pigs; brains, bones, entrails, and nerve tissue. Pickton made a steady income from the sale of these useless parts.

However, there seemed to be an extra ingredient to both the food being provided to fatten the pigs, and the remains being sent to the rendering plant. The thing is, there was an increasingly-worrying amount of women disappearing in and around the area where the farm and Palace stood, and though at first it didn't raise many alarms, it would ultimately be the first sign of something foul occurring underfoot.

In reality, the farmer had already found a new hobby besides organizing raves and slaughtering hogs, one which was much more twisted and darker...

## True Nature

The Piggy's Palace, already surrounded with controversy, would soon become too much for the Pickton's to handle. Its seedy nature was starting to become more public than the brothers had wished, and questions were being asked. The thing is, the brothers loved catering to every visitor's tastes, and these were typically activities and habits which sat on the wrong side of the law. David Francis himself was involved in a sexual assault in 1992, fined $1,000 and given 30 days probation for attacking a woman in his trailer at the pig farm. He had also been sued twice for traffic accidents in 1988 and 1991. The brothers were shady characters who had grown more morally-corrupt when the money started rolling in.

This led to two things — one, the parties at the Palace getting out of control, and two, Pickton's first close encounter with the law.

Robert frequently picked up and spent time with prostitutes from Vancouver's downtown eastside, sometimes finding his preferred sex workers as close as a single block away from the rendering plant, in an area known as Low Track. This area of the city is less glamorous, a skid row of ugly hotels and shady drug addicts, where pimps and prostitutes roamed free in broad daylight. It is said to be the poorest area in all of Canada. Rob picked the prostitutes up on the street, took them to cheap hotels and had sex with them and finally consumed illegal drugs that he was provided with from shadier individuals in town. Pickton continually made contact with said prostitutes and hired them to entertain guests at his party, but deep down he had another hateful, destructive plan in his mind. Make no mistake; Robert Pickton was a violent, angry man who wanted to hurt women. He abused the prostitutes he picked up, and was already on his way to becoming a serial killer by the first time he was first arrested.

On March 23, 1997, Pickton was charged with the attempted murder of Wendy Lynn Eistetter, a prostitute who he had stabbed several times after having an altercation with her at the farm. She was found half-naked and covered in blood walking late at night on a nearby street, the semi-conscious sex-worker desperately telling police that the pig farmer had handcuffed and then wounded her while she'd attempted to escape. In an act of desperation, she had succeeded in disarming and stabbing the assailant before getting out of the farm. They were both treated at the same hospital, just a few rooms apart. Unfortunately for Wendy, a few weeks before trial her case was dropped and Robert was set free — she was a drug addict, and it was her word against the local millionaire's. His crime was soon forgotten, and the pig farmer's feeling of invincibility grew.

Shortly after this event, Port Coquitlam officials paid the Pickton's a visit and saw the state of the siblings' farm, noting they had widely neglected the agriculture for which the land had been zoned, and were spending all of their time and resources on the 'altered farm building,' which now served to hold dances, parties, and other events instead of its original function. The Pickton's were sued, but after appearing in court they believed the authorities were full of empty threats and hot air. It didn't take long for them to continue throwing their grand parties which drew as many as 1,800 guests to them. The Port Coquitlam authorities didn't enjoy being ignored, and after a particularly large party on December 31, 1998, the brothers received an injunction which banned future parties at the Piggy's Palace and authorized police to arrest any person who was caught attending events within the walls of the building. Financial statements were looked at after news of the injunction became public, and it became clear the society's non-profit status was being taken advantage of for Robert and David's gain, so the government removed it in 2000. The Palace became little more than a pretty building, and the Pickton's had to find other activities to participate in during their leisure time.

While these were big problems for the Pickton's, there was something much worse happening behind the scenes, which would start to tear open the cracks of a terrible secret they'd been hiding.

Several people worked on their farm, Palace and other properties, and among them was a 37-year-old named Bill Hiscox. He had formerly been an addict who had turned to alcohol and drugs after losing his wife, but his foster sister — Robert William Pickton's girlfriend — had helped land him a job at P&B Salvage, a Pickton-owned business southeast of Vancouver. From day one, Hiscox felt on edge within the Pickton's employment, and remembered the terror he'd felt when entering their farm to pick up a paycheck and standing face-to-face with a 600-pound boar which served as a 'patrol dog,' even joining the dogs in their routine, and chased anyone it didn't recognize.

Hiscox was the first person to begin suspecting Robert's involvement in the case of missing women in the Vancouver area, the worker having seen a mound of women's purses and ID's in Pickton's trailer. The stabbing of Wendy Lynn Eistetter only made Hiscox more suspicious, and he decided to go to the authorities. Police greeted him and sat him down for a recorded statement, during which he spoke of Robert's suspicious behavior, his frequent visits to downtown for girls and his secrecy. Detectives took Bill's words seriously, and immediately one of them accompanied him to take a look at the farm.

Unfortunately, despite two police searches which would soon follow, nothing of interest was found, and

Bill's statement on the Pickton's simply served to put them on a list of 'persons of interest' in the case of the missing females.

The number of missing women continued to grow, the task force set to find them expanded greatly in size and more officers and resources were pooled into the investigation to obtain some results.

Pickton didn't suffer any consequences and was able to continue his life as if nothing had happened at all. It was, again, another hurdle he had overcome, and it allowed him to feel the relief of staying out of trouble.

The truth is that Robert William Pickton, or *'Willie'* to friends, was certainly behind many of the disappearances and was taking the lives of innocent street-workers. Robert Pickton, a millionaire-slash-pig-farmer was a serial killer…

…and it would be a while before he was caught.

## Finding the Culprit

The investigation's scope grew wider and the number of officers grew; they needed to find out what was going on, and they needed to find out fast. Missing women could easily mean dead women, and police were discovering links to missing person's cases from as far as the mid-1980s. Suspects were kept under discreet surveillance, but nothing the police attempted brought about any results in the investigation.

Despite the increasing focus on the disappearing women, their numbers continued to grow from 1997 onwards, and only then did the police realize how serious the situation was. Something must be said before we continue, Low Track isn't the kind of place where people are closely-watched or taken care of. It is British Columbia's rock-bottom drug scene; a place where heroin and crack cocaine flowed freely from the hands of motorcycle gangs and the Asian cartels, who were as ruthless with each other as they were with their clients — both became their victims, one way or another.

Low Track is also one of the worst prostitute-ridden areas in Canada, boasting the highest HIV infection rate in the entire continent of North America; one fourth of the neighborhood testing positive in 1997, and girls as young as 11-years-old ply their trade as sex-workers who sell their bodies for ten to twenty bucks; an amount which can allow them to get their hands on a quick fix of drugs to get them through the day. Most prostitutes in the area are Aboriginal, having been born outside of Vancouver and lured to the city with the promise of a better life. When they started to disappear from 1983 onwards, it took people a while to realize — or perhaps, it took people a while to *care.*

It took a long list of possible victims — written by an Aboriginal group and sent to the authorities in 1998 — for a Detective named Dave Dickson to actually take a step forward and offer to launch his own investigation; the one which would at least solve the mystery partially.

Vancouver police reviewed 40 cases of unsolved disappearances, dating back to 1971. It wasn't easy work, because sex-workers generally changed their name and location with time, evading their past with increasing persistence as the years pass. Soon, though, the detectives were able to narrow down their search to the cases of those women who'd disappeared from Low Track.

By 2001, the investigators had compiled a document of over 54 missing women who had disappeared between 1983 and the present year, their task force consisted of 85 investigators, divided in their opinions: some believed there was a serial killer out there who was taking these women and disposing of their bodies in the local area, the others thought that many of the cases were in fact women who had left the area or died in isolated incidents. The serial killer theory turned out to be the losing argument, and the inspector who insisted on standing by it was dismissed from the Vancouver P.D.

Media attention was growing, and some outlets were quick to put forward the — yet unconfirmed — statement that a serial killer was taking lives of women in the Downtown Eastside area. The lack of forensic evidence didn't help, and Canadian laws stated that missing person cases without evidence of foul play were not tracked, leading to the detectives having more trouble finding any data. Relatives, hospitals, drug rehab facilities, and other institutions were visited to seek the possibility of shedding light, and 16 new unsolved prostitute murders were discovered.

It wasn't all bad news, however, as five of the 54 women were found, dead or alive. Three were found living in other cities, completely oblivious to the fact that they had been on a list of missing persons; two had died in the following years and were finally accounted for.

The names of suspects began to grow, and police started looking at those men who had already struck against women of the local area. A man named Michael

Leopold was the first to appear on the list, a violent client who had beat a sex-worker and attempted to force a rubber ball down the woman's throat until she screamed and managed to escape. The investigators absolved him of the recent disappearances, but he received a 14-year prison sentence for his crime not long after.

Barry Niedermier, 43-years-old, was the next man in their sights. Police knew of his conviction for having pimped out a 14-year-old, and also of his violent attacks on Low Track prostitutes in the year 2000. Eventually, however, he was named only a person of interest and not a suspect because none of his assault victims were on the list of missing persons.

Yet another suspect was an unidentified rapist who had committed his assault on a Low Track hooker within his car, and claimed he had sexually assaulted and killed other women while the attack took place. This man was never captured or even named.

A bigger name, Gary Ridgeway — the Green River Killer, who kidnapped and/or killed 49 women — was suggested as a suspect, but no evidence linked him to Low Track or its missing person cases. A convicted rapist named Ronald McCauley was also investigated, his crimes having taken place in North Vancouver. He remained in the police's sight for a while, until they shifted their attention.

More and more suspects were either ruled out or kept under watch, but they were no closer to catching the killer.

Vancouver Police continued their work, and before long made some progress. Missing persons were reported more often and quicker than before — in one case, a woman had been missing a decade and a half before she was actually reported as disappeared — and there were signs that more people were paying attention to the women who were at risk. At the same time, the killer was starting to strike faster and more frequently than ever, and the pressure mounted for investigators. Women disappeared in intervals as frequent as five to seven days from each other, and the population was terrified. *Who was doing this, and why?* They asked. It was a shocking situation, but it was about to end.

## A Killer Captured

On February 6, 2002, four years after the investigation had begun; police executed a search warrant for illegal firearms at the Pickton property. They had been tipped off by somebody close. It would be the third time the farm had been searched, but this time the Pickton's were put in custody and officers realized there were links between Robert and David and the missing women. So it was later that same day, the Vancouver Police Department secured a second court order to search for personal items belonging to missing prostitutes.

Possessions belonging to a woman on the list were discovered in a trailer on the farm, and despite having been released for the weapons offence after being charged, Robert was arrested again on February 22 and charged with two counts of first degree murder in the deaths of Sereena Abotsway, missing since August 2001, and Mona Wilson, missing since November 30, 2001. On April 2nd, three more charges were added for the murders of Jacqueline McDonell, Diane Rock, and Heather Bottomley, and as more and more evidence sprang up, it took Robert Pickton past 15 murder counts in October — the most for a serial killer in Canada's history — and up to a shocking 27 murder charges by May, 2005.

Excavations had been made on the land since the discovery of the woman's belongings, and DNA was found in several parts of the farm, as well as a small amount of human remains. Detectives were puzzled as to where the bodies of his victims had gone, but they soon found the answer. Now, reader, do you remember that rendering plant that we described earlier?

Well, Pickton regularly stopped by the plant and unloaded the barrels of remains himself, barehanded, with workers watching horrified as he manipulated rotten pig gore with his own hands and refused the gloves they offered him. Despite authorities attempting to calm down the general populace by denying this, Robert himself would later confess that he disposed of many victims with the remains of hogs he had slaughtered, as well as fed them to the pigs he cooked at parties. In other words, people living in or passing through Vancouver who had eaten the locally-produced pork or used any of West Coast Reduction Ltd products had come into contact with the remains of dead prostitutes.

As for the confession itself, it was an amusing slip-up by the serial killer. During his arrest in February 22, he shared his cell with a man who said he was in there for murder. They talked a lot, enough for Robert's cell mate to finally earn some trust from the pig farmer. Eventually, the man spoke of how he had killed someone with a pickaxe and how he was going down for it. Until that moment, Pickton had been holding back on the truth and had insisted he hadn't done anything, but in an act of extreme stupidity on his part, he opened up and confessed to having used a rendering plant to dispose of the bodies. While his cell mate listened in awe, Pickton added that he was *'gonna do one more and make it fifty,'* making it clear that he had killed forty-nine women on his farm. He mentioned how he had used syringes filled with antifreeze to kill some of them, and regretted having turned sloppy at the end. Finally, he spoke of all of the guns and ammo he had; a big collection, to be fair, and showed pride in what he'd done.

He made a massive mistake, however.

His cell mate was an *undercover police officer.* He was actually being *filmed* as well. Robert Pickton had screwed up, bad.

His trial began on January 30, 2006, in New Westminster. The killer immediately pleaded not guilty to 27 charges of first-degree murder in the Supreme Court of British Columbia. A publication ban was set until January 2007, when the citizens of Canada were finally allowed to read the details of the ongoing trial.

The populace was horrified with what they learned: skulls cut in half with human parts inside them, remains found in a bag, human bones found in a slaughterhouse and a loaded .22 revolver with a dildo wrapped over the barrel and syringes with blue cleaning materials were just some of the things detectives had discovered during the investigation.

A videotape was released of Pickton's friends describing the man's method of murder: one spoke of how Pickton had boasted of killing a female heroin addict by injecting her with windshield washer fluid, while another recounted how Pickton had handcuffed and strangled a woman, before bleeding her, gutting her and feeding her corpse to his pigs.

It took a few more months, but finally the moment arrived: on December 11, 2007, Robert Pickton was sentenced to life with no possibility of parole for 25 years, the maximum punishment for second-degree murder. The judge, Justice Williams, said that Pickton was murderous, senseless, and despicable in what he had done to his victims.

He remains incarcerated to this day in a federal prison.

Robert Pickton was an atypical serial killer in that he was fully able to lead a normal life without letting his desires take over him until the very end, and he was able to dispose of his victims in a way that not even the most cautious killer can. He seemed very proud of what he had done in private, similarly to most murderers, but publicly denies to this day his involvement in the crimes.

The Vancouver Police Department received a civil lawsuit by the families of victims in 2013 for failing to protect them, and was forced to pay a settlement in March 2014, where each of their children received $50,000.

Pickton's brother, David, has since been interviewed, and spoke with disappointment of his brother's acts, stating that Robert was always slow but never violent, and that he felt like he had never actually known his sibling as he thought he'd had.

Perhaps he's being honest, or perhaps…

…perhaps Robert Pickton was part of something much bigger, and more men were involved and are still out there…*Food for thought.*

# TWO

-----------------------------

## The Scarborough Rapist

Love is a beautiful thing, an emotion that pushes us to greater things and fills us with the warmth that no other sensation has the possibility of doing. It is wonderful, magical, and so imperfect in its flaws that we associate it with the sole fact of being a human being.

To love is to live, and every person who has loved in their life is aware of how high it can take you and how happy you can feel when your heart is beating for somebody else.

But what happens when that love is corrupted with murderous desires?

When the warmth and feelings of company are poisoned with obsession, lies, and the necessity to satisfy each other even in the most terrible things?

Love can be beautiful, but it can be incredibly dangerous and horrific when corrupted. Love can make people do the nicest things, but it can also make them commit the most terrible acts.

Our next killer is not only the second in our book, but the second Canadian, and an example of how bad childhood traumas can affect a growing human being, turning them into the worst type of monsters to walk amongst us.

It is time to tell the story of **Paul Bernardo**, the *'Schoolgirl Killer,'* and his accomplice, wife and greatest love, **Karla Homolka**.

## Born into Disorder

Scarborough, a rapidly growing administrative district within the Canadian city of Toronto, Ontario, is a diverse and multicultural community with plenty of natural landmarks, boasting the reputation of being the greenest part of the entire city, having less violent crime than its neighbor districts and the coexistence of many different minority groups and religions. It is generally a peaceful, safe place to live in, and life can be quite comfortable for its inhabitants.

Our killer was born into this tranquil district of the Ontario province on August 27, 1964, to Kenneth Bernardo and Marilyn Eastman. They were wealthy, but things weren't peaceful or normal at home; in fact, they were a complete chaos.

Kenneth was the son of an English woman and an Italian immigrant, who had established a successful business selling tiles and marble, but he was an abusive, sexual deviant who would go on to regularly abuse both Marilyn and Paul. Meanwhile, Marilyn had been adopted by a rich lawyer named Gerald Eastman and his wife, Elizabeth, who raised her in a stable household.

The couple wasn't exactly dying to spend the rest of their lives together — Marilyn married Kenneth because her father rejected another boyfriend she had introduced to him as her possible husband. This discontent continued into Kenneth and Marilyn's relationship, and while he continually abused and disrespected her, Marilyn began to see her ex-boyfriend regularly, eventually becoming pregnant and giving birth to both a son and a daughter. Paul was born of this union, though Kenneth accepted to be registered as his biological father on the birth certificate.

When Paul was 11, in 1975, his father fondled a girl and was charged with child molestation. This wasn't news to Paul, as he was aware his father had been sexually abusing his young sister as well. Marilyn soon grew so detached and depressed that she moved into the basement of their home, very rarely interacting with her husband, son or daughter again. She had grown morbidly obese and no longer took of herself; she was now a shell of what she had once been.

Somehow, though, Paul managed to smile through all of these troubles. He was described as someone who was always happy: a cute, good-looking boy with good manners, and good marks at school. He even served as a counselor for the Boy Scouts, and the younger children loved the way he treated them.

Business and money came easy to him, and he had all the signs of becoming a successful businessman in the future. He was the local role model, and nobody could have guessed he would grow up to become a rapist and murderer. Paul Bernardo was, by all accounts and unlike his father, one of the good guys.

All of that would change when his mother confessed, immediately after an argument, that he and his sister were products of an extra-marital affair, even producing a photograph of his real father to reinforce the point. This broke Paul, and he suddenly lost all respect for his mother. He lashed out, calling her a slob and a whore, which she responded by reminding him he was a bastard. It was the last straw — Paul officially despised both of his parents and felt he needed to get away from it all.

His first step into darkness was to spend increasingly more time with rough, neighborhood boys, who poisoned him with their negative habits and criminal activities. Some were even thieves, and they spoke very badly of women and the more vulnerable members of society. It ultimately changed him considerably after he'd previously been a morally-correct youngster.

In his late teenage years and early twenties, Paul and a friend were recruited into Amway, a famous sales business, after graduating from Sir Wilfrid Laurier Collegiate Institute. It changed his life for the worse. Amway didn't really represent a huge source of income for Paul Bernardo, but it certainly changed his mindset forever. He closely studied the books and tapes sold by the company, and began to apply his lessons to real life.

In the books, writers spoke of a philosophy for instant success which involved exaggeration and even fabricating life stories. Paul and his buddy used this to seduce many women during their night ventures through the city, and eventually Bernardo became an expert manipulator.

But there was something else…

Bernardo hadn't just learned how to pick women up and get them to open their legs; he had also begun to develop a twisted side to his sexual desires. He wanted submissive women, to which he could perform forceful acts of fellatio and anal sex. Beatings and humiliations were also common in his brief, unstable relationships.

Paul was falling to the darkness, just like his father. He was becoming a monster…

…and nobody was going to stop him until it was too late.

## Like Father, Like Son

When Paul entered the University of Toronto, the corruption of his darkened conscious reached new heights.

He and his friend Van Smirnis were looking for quick, big money for their tastes — both of them needed it to support their expensive habits. They immediately began to smuggle and traffic in stolen goods, often taking cigarettes across the border and stealing license plates from random cars to keep their business going. Paul also looked for other easy, illegal ways to get some cash when he wasn't making any trips.

He soon graduated and began to work as a junior accountant for a local company, just like his father had. There was something in his mind, however. He wanted to make his fantasies come true, whatever the cost. He was a hungry sex addict and wanted to experiment beyond the borders of a relationship: he wanted to act out his fantasies on unwilling strangers. And not just strangers; Paul had a taste for younger girls and virgins, women who were 'pure' in his eyes. The idea of defiling virgin women was thrilling to him, and it soon began to take hold of his thoughts more and more.

In 1987, Paul Bernardo's obsession with committing an assault came to fruition.

On May 4th, Paul followed a 21-year-old Scarborough woman home. She had been on the same bus as him as he cruised through town waiting for a victim.

As the unnamed victim descended from the public transportation, he walked behind her and out of sight, waiting for her to reach the darkness of the porch of her parent's house. He took her away into the shadows. She resisted, but he was stronger, and for one whole hour Paul raped her again and again — both vaginally and anally — before leaving the sobbing, terrified woman to pick up the pieces.

The attack left Paul with an excited feeling of satisfaction, and he felt like it was something he had to start doing more often. It didn't take him long to repeat his crime on another victim: just ten days later, when he spotted another victim on one of his late night bus trips. He also followed her home and assaulted her as she entered the backyard of her parent's home. The ordeal again lasted an entire hour, and Paul successfully escaped.

On July 17, a confident Paul repeated his method. He followed his victim-to-be, but this time the woman was not so submissive. She fought back fiercely and managed to cause enough noise for Paul to flee the scene. She would be among the minority of the women attacked by Paul Bernardo to actually escape the sexual assault.

On September 29 of the same year, he committed his most daring assault yet.

Having already set his eyes on her on a previous occasion, Paul staked out the house where a pretty 15-year-old lived, waiting for the moment where he could strike and take her as he pleased. He watched the lights go off inside the home, one by one, and prepared himself.

Paul broke into the home with ease, climbing up to the girl's bedroom and found her on her bed. He jumped on her, covered her mouth with his hand, and threatened her with a knife as he bit her ear and face, leaving bruises. As he proceeded to finish what he started, the victim's mother heard something and entered the room, screaming desperately at the mystery attacker and forcing him to escape the scene.

Funnily enough, a 19-year-old man known as Anthony Haanmayer was convicted for the assault and even served a sixteen-month prison sentence, eventually being exonerated when Bernardo finally admitting to the crime in 2006.

Things were going smoothly enough for Paul, but they were about to get even better. Thing is, Paul Bernardo was about to meet his dream counterpart; a woman who would take his fantasies to a new level and bring a reign of terror to the Scarborough district.

*Enter Karen Homolka.*

## A Couple to Die For

Karla Leanne Homolka was born the 4<sup>th</sup> of May, 1970, in Port Credit, Ontario, to Karel Homolka and Dorothy Seger. She was the eldest of three sisters; Lori, born in 1971, and Tammy, 1975, and had Czech roots on her father's side. He had come from Czechoslovakia to start a new life as a salesman.

She'd had a normal, happy childhood filled with great memories, and showed a bright, intelligent side that surprised her parents and teachers. Although she suffered from asthma that was triggered by feelings of excitement or fear, it didn't affect her overall health or happiness.

As she grew, however, signs began to show that she was becoming an obsessive perfectionist, and that she was extremely bossy with her fellow classmates and friends. She loved animals, but a friend recalled that she once deliberately killed a hamster by throwing him out of a window. She also loved Barbie dolls and wanted to be just like the plastic heroines, finding a handsome partner and moving into a big, fancy house.

The years passed and Karla started to change dramatically, and eventually she and her closest friends formed an exclusive group called *'The Diamond Club,'* a clique that had the final goal of finding rich, good-looking older men so that they could get engaged; *get the diamond*, marry and live happily ever after.

Although her childhood had been normal, her teenage years were not, and her father began drinking a bit too much, causing him to turn abusive with his wife and daughters.

Unlike Paul, Karla and her sisters fought back, and it became a constant power struggle that weighed down on the young girl, causing her to become depressive. It was this constant battle of control and the fact that she had increasingly strong desires of bondage and pain that made her seek out someone who was like-minded.

*And she found him.*

In October, 1987, while Paul, 23 years of age, was still in the first year of his Scarborough rape spree, he met Miss Homolka, 17 at the time, at a Toronto restaurant and immediately sparks began to fly between the two. She had found her handsome, rich Ken who could give her what she wanted in bed, and he had found the woman to control and dominate as he pleased; the partner in crime that would motivate him to continue his terrible crimes.

Even after meeting her, he continued raping strangers in the area — although Karla cared little and called it *'going hunting,'* even asking for the ugly details — and in December of the same year he claimed two more victims. The first was a 15-year-old, who Bernardo assaulted during one hour after following her home. Metropolitan Toronto Police finally caught signs of the pattern, and the next day issued a warning to women traveling alone through the city at night.

The second victim was a 17-year-old. He used a knife to threaten her and keep her quiet, and when he was done he was gone. This rape would prove to be the one that lifted him to his infamous reputation as *'The Scarborough Rapist.'* A facial composite was released of his face, although it didn't get anyone closer to arresting him.

He didn't attack again until April of 1988, when he raped for the fifth time, this time taking advantage of a 17-year-old for 45 minutes. The next month, he had a close call which almost led to his capture. He had been hiding in wait for a victim near a bus shelter when a Metro Toronto investigator spotted him under a tree and began to pursue him. The rapist managed to escape, and only five days later, on May 30, Bernardo raped an 18-year-old. This time, he made sure to change location, committing his crime in Mississauga, 40 kilometers southwest of Scarborough. It was a brutal rape which involved a beating and forceful anal penetration once the young woman had been subdued.

His next attack took place four months later and back in Scarborough, the district where he'd caused so much grief. It was his seventh attempted rape in the area, although it was unsuccessful — the victim managed to fight him off during her desperation, and in his fury he sliced her thigh and buttock. The ensuing cut would require 12 stitches.

A day after an additional rape on November 16, 1988, the Metro Police formed a task force in an attempt to capture the dreaded Scarborough Rapist. Paul was not deterred by the increased police attention and he attempted to rape again on December 28, his would-be victim screaming loud enough for a neighbor to hear and chase him off. He waited long before the next attack in June 1989, but it again was unsuccessful. This time, his victim managed to scratch his face.

Paul lay low for 2 months, and on August 15, he attacked with a careful viciousness that ensured his success: he spent the night before the attack stalking his victim outside the window of her apartment and planned his attack before it took place. When she arrived home on the day of the assault, he pounced on her and forced her inside. What followed were two hours of painful, forceful penetration. It was the eighth victim he'd raped.

On November 21 and December 22, Bernardo attacked once more, a 15-year-old and a 19-year-old, respectively. It wasn't until May 26, 1990, after his eleventh rape, that Paul's horrific spree finally came to an end. His victim endured an hour of humiliation, but she was able to remember his face clearly. After suffering the ordeal, she went to the police with her memory still vivid of the events and of the man who had committed the terrible crime.

Two days later, the computer composite photograph was released by the police, and published in Toronto and the local area.

It took only two months for Bernardo to be brought in after he was reported by an anonymous tip to be very similar to the man in the image.

*Was it finally time for the* Scarborough Rapist *to go to prison?*

As history has already told us, it wasn't. In fact, Paul was going to go through a process of transformation before it was over...

## A Rapist Reinvented

Over 130 suspects were made to submit their DNA, but Bernardo wasn't just any simple suspect. He had been identified not only by a bank worker as similar to the composite image, but by the sister of Van Smirnis, a young woman named Tina. She told police that he had already been called in for a previous rape investigation, but had never gone to the interview. Paul also regularly boasted about his sex life and spoke of how he loved rough and anal sex. Tina Smirnis suffered from a stilted speech condition and had difficulty explaining what she wanted to say, but ultimately the detectives decided to give her word a chance and called Paul in for an interview.

It took place on November 20, 1990. Paul entered the police station and voluntarily provided the requested samples for testing. When asked why he thought they'd called him in, he admitted that he had a resemblance with the composite image. He dominated the interview and didn't seem to be nervous at all; Tina would ultimately look like a doubtful source of credibility and someone who was probably trying to collect the reward. The rapist was released the following day.

After his release, Bernardo met with Homolka at her home in St. Catharine's and assured her that he wasn't the Scarborough Rapist. He requested to move in with her, and she was thrilled at the idea. In February of the following year, 1991, they would begin living together.

During the year 1990, between the rapes, Paul had spent a lot of time with Karla Homolka's family, getting to know them better and earning their trust. He was engaged to Karla, but he had an attraction towards her younger sister, Tammy. Tammy was a younger, virgin version of Karla, and this *'purity'* made Paul lustful for her. He regularly flirted with her and peered into her window. On occasion, he masturbated beside her as she slept. Karla, always so willing to please him, began to hatch a plan to make her precious Paul a happy man.

She had been working at an animal clinic and had learned how to use sedatives to put them to sleep. In her mind, she could do the same to Tammy and keep her knocked out while Paul took advantage of her and took the virginity that Karla herself hadn't been able to give him.

So they planned and planned, and on December 23, 1990 — six months before the couple's marriage — they decided it was time. Karla had stolen Halothane from the clinic, an anesthetic agent used for sedating animals for surgery. Tammy was invited to drink with them, and she accepted, unaware that it had been laced with the chemical compound. Once she was unconscious, she was taken to the basement and videotaped as Paul raped her. Karla was next, performing oral sex on her sister to please her fiancé's fantasies.

However, something went wrong. Before they could finish the filming, Tammy began to vomit. The two desperate lovers tried hard to revive her and called 911, but suddenly they noticed she wasn't breathing. In a last act of desperation, they dressed her and themselves, hid the camera and placed her in her bedroom. She was found there by the paramedics, who took her to St. Catharine's General Hospital...

...only to discover that she was dead. It was too late. After a visit from a coroner, it was declared that

Tammy had died from choking on vomit after consuming alcohol. Karla did not show any remorse for what she'd participated in, and would even subsequently dress in her dead sister's clothes while Paul had sex with her.

A similar event would occur right before their wedding on June 7, 1991, when Homolka brought a 15-year-old girl to their new home after drugging her with Halcion. When Paul asked her who the girl was, Karla replied that she was his *'wedding gift.'* A virgin, just as he liked them, and a Tammy lookalike.) They proceeded to film the ensuing vaginal and anal rape that followed once the minor was in their bedroom. When she woke up, the girl, known as *'Jane Doe,'* was unaware of what had happened. She would visit the home again in August and also stop breathing after being drugged and raped, but survived the ordeal.

The next victim was not so fortunate.

The couple had married in a grand wedding which Paul treated more like a business opportunity — amassing thousands in gifts and donations from the guests — than a ceremony. Paul wanted a wife that wouldn't just 'love and cherish' him, but also 'obey' his every will.

Suddenly, his will was to put another young girl through a horrible ordeal.

Leslie Mahaffy was a rebellious young girl. She regularly skipped school, had promiscuous sex, and even got caught shoplifting once. On the night of Friday, June 14, 1991, she went out and stayed past her curfew. She arrived home at 2 in the morning to find her home locked and nobody there to receive her. This caused Leslie to look for her best friend for help, but the girl told her she'd get in trouble if she opened the door at that hour. Leslie decided to go back home.

She would encounter Bernardo on her way back, carelessly asking him for cigarettes, and her life would change forever.

After pulling a knife on her and forcing her into his car, Paul drove back home, where he would strip, blindfold and tie Leslie up until Karla arrived. The two sexually abused and tortured Mahaffy while videotaping it all. Paul's anal penetration causing the girl to scream. They committed the acts while listening to music, and eventually the attack ceased temporarily. In this time, Leslie made the mistake of telling Bernardo that the blindfold was slipping. Both killers knew what this meant. *She could have possibly seen their faces.*

55

The lovers' story differs at this step of the ordeal: Karla would later confess that Bernardo strangled Leslie to death, while Paul claims that Homolka injected her with a lethal dose of Halcion. Either way, Leslie Mahaffy was dead the following day. The Bernardo's had dinner with Karla's family while Leslie's body lay in the basement.

Unaware of how to dispose of a body, Paul suggested they dismember Leslie and encase each piece in cement so the pieces would sink in a body of water. Agreeing on the plan, Paul quickly went to a hardware store for several bags of cement — foolishly keeping the receipts — and picked up his grandfather's circular saw so they could successfully cut her to pieces.

They dumped the blocks into Lake Gibson, taking several trips to finally finish disposing of the corpse. One block, however, did not sink, and a father and son discovered it on June 29 of the same year. Leslie's braces were instrumental in identifying her.

The couple's third victim was 15-year-old Kristen French, an attractive and popular teenager, who studied at a local Catholic School. She had the misfortune of walking back home while the couple were driving around, looking for a next victim. They lured her over to their car with ease, simply asking her for directions which she was eager to give. Karla kept her busy with a map, asking for directions, while Paul walked around the vehicle and prepared himself.

As Kristen was distracted, he put a knife to her throat and forced her into the front seat of the car. Karla sat in the back, pulling on French's hair to keep her in control.

Kristen's death sentence had already been signed — she had seen Paul and Karla and knew what their house and car looked like. Even so, the couple would not reveal this to the girl to keep her cooperative all the while.

Kristen was held for three whole days — the entire Easter weekend — and both Bernard and Homolka videotaped themselves as they tortured, raped, and sodomized the young girl, constantly forcing her to drink copious amounts of alcohol and submit to Paul's every will. Meanwhile, French's parents had already suspected foul play and informed the authorities: the Niagara Regional Police Service assembled a team and followed Kristen's route, finding several witnesses who had seen the abduction take place. One of the girl's shoes at the scene confirmed the kidnapping.

The unfortunate girl was extremely cooperative, believing that she could ensure her survival that way. Paul was extremely sadistic toward her, even going as far as urinating on her and squatting over her face to defecate on it to no success. All of it was videotaped, before either Paul, according to Homolka, strangled her with his bare hands during seven minutes; or Karen, according to Paul, beat her with a rubber mallet and finally put a noose around the girl's neck and strangled her.

French's nude body was found in a ditch about 45 minutes from St. Catharines on April 30, 1992. She had been washed and her hair was cut off. Homolka would subsequently testify that she'd done this to make identification more difficult.

The circumstances which led to Karla and Paul's arrests were complicated, but as with every villain and villainess, the bad guy always gets what's coming to him. And for two horrible human beings such as Bernardo and Homolka, this meant great news for the city of Toronto, Ontario.

# A Deal with the Devil

On the 15th of May, 1992, the Green Ribbon Task Force was formed to investigate the murders of both Leslie Mahaffy and Kristen French. Two of Bernardo's friends came forward on different occasions and offered their theories that he was involved in at least one of the rapes and murders, if not both. The couple had already begun a legal process to have their surname changed to Teale, the name of a television serial killer which they admired. Bernardo was interrogated briefly and admitted to having been questioned for the Scarborough Rapist crimes, but nothing came of it.

Paul had submitted DNA samples two years earlier, and it wasn't until December of 1992 when the Centre of Forensic Sciences began to test them to check for a result. At the end of the aforementioned month, Paul made a grave mistake which would accelerate his fall — he took a domestic beating too far and brutally slammed a flashlight into Homolka's limbs and face over and over again, leaving her eyes heavily bruised. Although the woman would explain her injuries as having been the result of an automobile incident, nobody believed her, and her parents convinced her to go to the police after receiving hospital treatment. Bernardo was arrested and

59

later released, but he had now lost his closest ally and accomplice.

His downfall had begun.

In early 1993, Toronto police were informed that the DNA sample they'd received from Paul was a match to that of the Scarborough Rapist, and he was put under surveillance. Meanwhile, they interviewed Karla and tried to get something from her, but she was evasive and talked more of the abuse she'd suffered than what he had done in his spare time. The pressure would nonetheless weigh down on her, and she realized that the police had him cornered.

It was now or never for Karla: she either confessed and got a deal, or she went down with Paul. Karla Homolka loved Paul Bernardo, but she wasn't about to spend her life in prison for him.

The same night of the questioning, she spoke to her aunt and uncle about Paul and his rape spree as the Scarborough Rapist; her involvement with him in the Mahaffy and French rape/murders and the fact that the crimes had been taped. Karla sent a letter to her parents and remaining sister, Lori, admitting to Tammy's death and stating that Paul had threatened her into participating in the drug-fueled rape. She spoke to a lawyer not long after, and together they planned a way for her to get legal immunity in exchange for her cooperation.

And cooperate she did.

Karla testified against Bernardo at his trial, putting to bed his claims that the deaths had all been accidental. Prosecutors were horrified by what they saw in the videos, and some admitted they would have never allowed Homolka a plea bargain if they'd seen the videos before the trial began. She was given the infamous 12-year sentence for manslaughter in what was considered the worst plea bargain in Canada's history, and Paul was locked away for life, his only hope hanging from a thin thread in what is called the *faint hope clause.*

Karla has since been released, in 2005, and allowed to change her name. She moved to Guadeloupe in the Caribbean for a brief time but currently lives in Quebec, Canada, where she has been recently spotted volunteering at her children's elementary school. She is still hounded by the press and people who hate her, but shows a great deal of remorse and regret for what she did.

Bernardo continues to claim he's innocent in the crimes committed and has even written a book since his incarceration, a book that was quickly banned by big sellers but can be found on the Internet. It is still believed that Paul was involved in several other rapes and murders, but no concrete evidence has been found to link him to them.

Either way, due to his dangerous sex offender status, it is unlikely he will ever be released from prison. *Let him rot,* most would say.

Well said.

# THREE

----------------------------

## The Beast of the Mangroves

For our next tale, we must move to new countries on a new continent. Colombia, South America, home to over 49 million people and famous for its beautiful women, successful musicians, and Pablo Escobar's empire; and Ecuador, a land of rich ecology, diverse population and only country in South America to have accepted the U.S. Dollar as its currency.

*What is the link between these two nations?*

Well, when it comes to something related to our book, it's the fact that they were both killing grounds for our next murderer: **Daniel Camargo**.

Camargo was an absolute monster of a human being, the victim of extended childhood humiliations and abuse which turned him into a spiteful man who lived only to cause misery to his young female victims — a number which ranged from 71 to 150 — and a monster who felt no remorse whatsoever for the crimes he'd committed.

The next story is about the dreaded *Sadist of El Charquito,* a predator as ruthless as he was cruel and who possessed the cunning that only a cold-hearted villain like Camargo can use to their benefit; one which allowed him to escape an Alcatraz-like prison and disappear into the public once more like a ghost before he began to strike again...

...the time for our next gruesome murderer has come.

## A Broken Boy

Daniel Camargo Barbosa was born on January 22, 1930, in the Cundinamarca region within the territories of the Colombian Andes, a tropical section of the long mountain range in South America. His mother died when he was just one-years-old, and his father soon remarried, choosing a woman with fertility issues named Dioselina, who was frustrated at not being able to bear a female child and cruelly lashed out at young Daniel whenever she could: she would frequently stab his skin with needles without any provocation as a sick sort of punishment and whip him on the buttocks. On several other occasions, Dioselina forced him to dress as a girl and sent him to school; this caused him much distress and bullying from his peers.

While another child may have seeked out solace in his father, Camargo's, also called Daniel, was a violent alcoholic who neglected him and ignored the mistreatment his child was receiving from his new wife. He was excessively severe and distant, caring only for money and interacting with his son only to beat him for whatever reason he saw fit at that moment.

Daniel was left heavily traumatized and unstable after this treatment from his parents, especially from his stepmother. It changed him forever and woke a hatred within his young heart — he would state many years later that the woman who had raised him had probably suffered from some sort of disorder, which in her mind led her to believe she could turn him into a girl by dressing him up and treating him as one. Daniel added that his experiences with Dioselina had brought about an accumulation of hatred and resentment towards women which would become something far uglier in the future.

Despite the bullying and all the terrible things taking place back home, Camargo managed to become a distinguished student at the León XIII School in Bogota; demonstrating his intelligence by having an IQ of 116, although he had to prematurely quit his studies to help out at home when his family went through economical hardships, a turn in his life that made him even more bitter towards them.

Still, Daniel grew up and functioned, for all his resentment, as a normal human being. He learned how to lie and manipulate, and he wasn't seen as an outcast to the outside world like he was at home. Daniel began to work as a door-to-door salesman, which he was quite good at, discovering that he was very convincing and could gain the trust of his clients without much effort. He even began a de facto union with a client named Alcira Castillo in 1960 and had two children with her. They moved in together, but soon Daniel realized that he wasn't earning enough money to cover their expenses, so he robbed the shop of one of his clients and was caught and sent to a minimum security prison. He managed to escape, and was soon back home with Alcira as if nothing had happened.

Daniel lived with Alcira and their children for two years, but in 1962 he met a woman who he immediately fell in love with. Her name was Esperanza, and she would be the final reason a hate-filled Daniel turned into a rapist.

## The Last Straw

Daniel felt something strong for Esperanza, so strong in fact that he left Alcira and the kids behind to move in with his new love. She was 28-years-old and beautiful. Daniel saw her as a symbol of purity. He dreamed of marrying her and starting a new life at her side.

But things did not go that way at all.

She soon confessed to him that she was not a virgin at all, and Daniel was disappointed and confused. There was a fixation in Daniel for *'pure'* virgins, and it annoyed him to know that another man had taken her virginity. Furthermore, not long into their relationship,

Daniel found her in bed with another man and was left heartbroken.

Camargo had wanted to start a life with her and yet she had failed him, just like every other woman had done since his birth. He would state after his capture that he was crazily in love with Esperanza and didn't know what to do after discovering her infidelity, going as far as arguing with himself on what decision to make.

Finally, he knew what he had to do. In his mind, Esperanza could still remain at his side, but Daniel would require something from her. He would need her to give him something from other women she had not been able to give him herself.

Esperanza sat down with Daniel and expected the worst, knowing any normal man would have asked her to leave after what he'd found her doing…but Daniel was no normal man. She listened to his proposal: he would remain with her in exchange for her finding young virgin girls and bringing them to his apartment so that he could deflower them.

Although it was a tough request he was making, Esperanza was suffocating in guilt and accepted. It was a task she began almost immediately. Her modus operandi was to lure the girls back to the home under false pretenses and drug them with Secobarbital sleeping pills, allowing her partner to rape them while they slept.

Five girls were raped this way, although the fifth and final victim — a child — realized what had happened while she was unconscious and reported the crime to the police. Both Camargo and Esperanza were arrested and taken to separate prisons. Daniel sat in trial and on the 10th of April, 1964, was convicted of sexual assault. Camargo was sentenced to three years in prison, and initially he hoped to repent and mend his ways after realizing that the judge had been lenient.

Unfortunately for him, another judge would soon take over the case and found his predecessor's decision to be *too* lenient. Camargo's sentence was increased to eight years, and this time Daniel wasn't so content. He entered a furious rage at the decision, a rebellious anger growing in him that led Daniel to swear two things on that fateful day: one, he would never again trust in the justice system or the people that represented it; and two, every time he raped a girl in the future, he would ensure she could not report the crime to anyone.

He was going to kill every single one of his victims so that they couldn't speak about what had happened to them.

# Gorgona

Daniel served his full sentence and was released in 1972. Wanting to leave his homeland behind, he decided to move to Brazil, but didn't make it far. He was arrested a year later for being undocumented. Thanks to a delay in Colombia which meant that his criminal records arrived late, he was deported back to his country and released with a new, false identity.

Now back in Colombia, he decided that the best thing to do was to lay low and work on the streets as a television monitor vendor in Barranquilla, a large city in the north of the country.

One day, as he was walking past a school, Camargo spotted a 9-year-old girl who he admittedly 'fell in love with,' and who he wanted to have sex with at any cost. So he waited for her to exit her school, patiently thinking of what argument he'd convince her with to follow him. Whatever he said once the girl was out on the street, it worked. The youngster followed him to a nearby secluded area, where she realized in horror what was about to happen. Despite her tears and screams, Daniel deflowered the girl and proceeded to strangle her to death so that she was unable to turn him in afterwards.

Something must have spooked him — whether it was the area suddenly became busier or simply that he had never imagined how he'd feel after his first murder, but Daniel didn't even bury or conceal his victim's body well, instead simply leaving her body alongside the TV sets he'd been transporting with him all day. It would turn out to be a costly error. He returned the next day, hoping to get rid of the corpse and continue selling his TV's, but didn't realize he was being followed by a curious police officer who arrested him upon interrogating the rapist and seeing the body.

Colombian justice was not lenient this time; they knew what he'd done before and this latest crime was unforgivable. He had to be made an example of. And he was.

Isla Gorgona is an isolated island located 22 miles away from Colombia's western coast, a 4 by 2 mile expanse of mostly jungle, rocks, and many different species of snakes and reptiles. It was also the place the Colombian government decided in 1959 to build a penitentiary for the worst criminals in the country. Guards were ruthless and sadistic, and when they weren't making the prisoners' lives hell, the other inmates were. Anybody smart or brave enough to escape the well-guarded prison would first have to find a way to tackle the dangerous snakes surrounding it before then struggling against the strong currents of the Pacific Ocean on their way back to the mainland.

It was where the judge decided that the cold-hearted Camargo would serve his 25-year sentence.

*Only ten years would pass before he escaped.*

Daniel was a smart man; a very smart man in fact. He did not spend his time in prison simply sitting around and learning of ways to be a thug within the walls of the penitentiary. No, Daniel knew instead that he had to nurture his mind in the works of greats and, of course, find a way out of the prison. He did the former by openly reading authors such as Nietzsche, Freud, and Dostoievsky, while secretly studying the books that gave him information about the ocean currents around the island and navigation. He sat in his cell and planned a way out of the apparently inescapable prison, knowing that there surely could be a way out. It would come to him almost by accident.

Gorgona spent certain periods of the month unguarded, and many prisoners didn't even bother to leave the prison due to the added risk of being bitten by a snake or having an accident in the jungle. Daniel had no such fears and regularly left on long walks. On one of these walks, the prisoner spotted something and approached to confirm it was what he believed. *Yes,* he observed, *an abandoned boat...* A way to escaping Gorgona for good. Without a second thought, Daniel pushed the boat out to the ocean and jumped inside, paddling hard for hours through the discomfort of dehydration, hunger, and the burning sunlight until he reached the mainland. He didn't even stop to rest, quickly running south as fast as he could to reach the border with Ecuador, where he immediately began his next plan.

Meanwhile the Colombian press began to report about the killer's escape, but quickly discounted him as being a dead man, one outlet even going as far as confirming him to have been eaten by sharks at sea. Nobody believed that a man could handle the currents that surrounded the prison, and Daniel Camargo was quickly forgotten by all.

The killer was still at large and was now a species of ghost that nobody knew existed, having entered an entirely new country where nobody expected him to be. Daniel's savage wave of terror was only just beginning, and its shockwaves would tear the local communities apart.

## The Mangrove Beast

The first thing Daniel did as a free man was head to Quito, the capital. Although he had wanted to start a new life — and a killing spree — there, he immediately regretted it and decided to look for a warmer place where he could feel more at home. So it was on the 5th of December, 1984, just as Christmas approached, Daniel traveled by bus to the warmer and more populated city of Guayaquil. He abducted his first victim just 13 days later, on the 18th. It was another innocent nine-year-old, who the killer found alone on the streets of Quevedo. After raping her, he murdered her in cold blood and left her defiled body to be found by locals. The next day, he went on to abduct a ten-year-old, and then his real wave of rape-murders began.

The corpses of young, underage girls began to appear all over the surrounding areas, with signs of stabbing, machete slashes, strangling, and brutal rape. They almost always were found naked in bushy areas near water — hence his nickname. During this period,

Camargo was a homeless nomad, working at a local market helping out with carrying weight around and surviving on a salary of less than one US dollar. Sometimes, when things got tougher, he would sell the clothes and belongings of his victims to get by. He ate the cheapest food he could find; goat meat, and slept on park benches.

Camargo was a very successful criminal. Thanks to his choice of location to dump the corpses, forensic specialists were unable to find much in terms of evidence due to wild animals picking at the bodies and general humidity making them rot quicker than they would have in other climates. Furthermore, a local gang of savage rapists made it harder to pinpoint the crimes on somebody else. Who would believe it was a skinny, 5 foot 5 inch man in his 50's, anyway?

His modus operandi involved targeting lonely low-class women who were returning from school or work, his best weapon being his persuasion — '*I preferred to persuade than to threaten,*' he would later say — using subtle tactics such as telling girls he was a foreign minister looking for a pastor in the local land; offering jobs, money or gifts, or even simply asking for help in exchange for their trust. He would further reinforce this image of a trustworthy middle-aged man by walking in front of them until they were approaching the area that he'd use as the site for murder. If they refused to continue following him into the more secluded areas, Camargo was smart enough to let them go; but if they accepted, a brutal rape and murder would inevitably follow.

The defilement didn't end when his victims were dead, either. Daniel regularly took body parts or organs with him, making sure not only to keep physical trophies but to remember each and every girl's name so that they could accompany him even in death. He admitted that many of the things he did to the bodies was also part of his strategy to keep the police guessing, and he always carried a spare shirt to keep himself clean; the shirt he was wearing served the purpose of cleaning his hands of dirt and blood when necessary. Daniel was no common thug and even possessed a fluency in English and Portuguese, as well as his native Spanish, and he had an extremely healthy memory. It is reported that he could even recall the scars, tattoos, and moles on his victims' bodies, and regularly read books from famous authors when he wasn't busy murdering or working at the market.

Sexually, he was considered a chauvinist with an obsession for virginity and purity. He hated most non-virgin women and had a special disgust towards prostitutes, who he saw as filthy and full of sexually-transmitted diseases. He was also a sadist, confessing that he loved to have sex with virgins *'because they cried the most,'* and would target younger and more vulnerable women because of this. He would openly admit that his crimes were the result of years of humiliation.

Whatever led him to go on his gruesome killing spree, a varying number between 71 and 150 young women died at his hands, many of them found cut in pieces by the unknown killer. It wasn't until 1986 when he'd be stopped for his terrible acts, although it was arguably too late.

February 26, 1986. Camargo was leaving the scene where he had just raped and murdered nine-year-old Elizabeth Telpes. Two officers inside an Interpol patrol car spotted him behaving suspiciously and approached to ask him what he was carrying in his bag. Within, they found the bloody clothes of a little girl, shocking both officers for a moment before they saw something else: little Elizabeth's severed clitoris. He was immediately arrested, and despite giving a false name —

Manuel Bulgarin Solis — was later identified by a victim who had managed to escape.

The killer himself admitted to his crimes, calmly telling authorities that he had killed 72 girls in Ecuador since escaping from Isla Gorgona. He accepted to lead them to the places he had used to dump the bodies that had not yet been recovered, and the dismembered corpses of young girls were found. Soon, everyone wanted to interview him due to his lack of remorse and the ease with which he offered all the details the interviewers requested of him. On one particular occasion, someone asked him why he had removed the lungs and kidneys of a young girl after killing her. Daniel replied: *"That is a lie; if anything I took her heart because it's the organ of love."* Soon, however, he began to request money in exchange for interviews, and after requesting 250,000 Sucres for an interview, wasn't bothered again.

Camargo was sentenced to 25 years in prison in 1989, the maximum sentence available in Ecuador. He served his time alongside the famous *'Monster of the Andes,'* Pedro Alonso López, who is believed to have raped and killed over 300 girls in three South American countries. While imprisoned, Daniel converted to Christianity and tried to fix his ways.

It wouldn't save him.

On one tranquil Sunday in November 1994 as Daniel sat within his cell, a man named Geovanny Arcesio Noguera Jaramillo entered his cell, forcing him to his knees and pulling out a makeshift knife. *"Es la hora de la venganza,"* he growled; *time for revenge,* and immediately stabbed Camargo eight times, slicing the killer's ear off and walking outside to call the guards and reveal why he'd done it — his aunt had been one of Camargo's victims, and he had been waiting patiently for revenge for a while.

Camargo's body wasn't claimed and he was buried in a mass grave within Quito's El Batán cemetery.

Daniel Camargo was a very unique murderer compared to the rest we've read about until now. He knew what he was and he embraced it. He did not fear the consequences of what was coming once he was caught. He was smart, cultured, and overall, he was extremely resilient.

He was molded by hatred and allowed his anger to have free rein over his emotions, giving in to what the psychopathic desires told him in his head. Daniel Camargo was a true, honest killer.

And that's what makes him one of the most dangerous killers in Colombia's history, and the entirety of South America as well. May his kind never be seen again.

# FOUR

--------------------------

# Night Stalker

**P**sychologists and other experts of the human mind enjoy pinpointing the faults and childhood traumas that cause problems later on in the lives of their patients, often feeling satisfied when they are able to discover the cause to a mental disorder after extensively studying the patient like a lab rat within a scientist's care.

Some people, however, are too far gone in their twisted sickness to be able to identify just what went wrong with them during their growth into mental maturity.

**Richard Ramirez** was one such individuals; a ruthless, cruel creature of a man who took at least 14 lives in brutal ways during a killing spree in the mid-80's, and who was heavily invested in raping or torturing his victims before finishing them off and caring little for the age or vulnerability of the people he was murdering.

Fame always followed him; as the mysterious *Night Stalker* or as *Ricardo Leyva Muñoz Ramirez*, Richard was also surrounded by a level of notoriety that he himself helped spread — we're about to find out just what made him such a celebrity in the serial killer world.

Ladies and gentlemen, the *Valley Intruder* has just entered the building, and he's bringing all the carnage he created with him. *Get ready.*

## Origins of a Monster

Richard Ramirez, born Ricardo Leyva Muñoz Ramirez, and later Americanized to his latter name, was brought forth into the world on the 29th of February, 1960, in a Hispanic barrio within the history-rich city of El Paso in western Texas. He was born to Julian Tapia Ramirez and Mercedes Muñoz, two very hard working Mexican immigrants who already had four elder children; three boys, Ruben, Joseph and Robert, and a girl, Ruth. Mercedes worked at a boot factory but had to quit during her pregnancy of Richard due to the fumes in the warehouse making her feel weak and sick, almost making her lose the baby growing within her. This, as well as Richard being the youngest, made her cherish him more than any of the other kids she'd born with Julian, and soon he was adored by both Mercedes and the rest of the family.

Julian and Mercedes were responsible parents, always trying their best to keep things together in the family and working as hard as they could to keep their children happy. Furthermore, Mercedes was a Roman Catholic, and similarly influenced her children to follow the path of God as well. Unfortunately, however, Julian was as strict as he was correct, and he found it hard to control his temper when his wife or children made a mistake, often exploding in a violent rage and beating them savagely.

At the tender age of two, Richard suffered a terrible accident that may have been one of the triggers for his behavior further along in life; a tall dresser collapsed on the infant, cutting open a savage gash in his forehead which would require 30 stitches to close and causing a concussion. Again, this time at age 5, Richard was hit in the head by a swing at a park, and he would soon begin to suffer from epileptic seizures that persisted for a few years.

Whether these events were the causes for his behavior as a teen and adult, one may never know, but Richard begun to get involved with crime at a very early age, also beginning to smoke marijuana at the premature age of 10. He also spent more and more time with his cousin Miguel "Mike" Ramirez, a decorated Green Beret veteran who had fought in the Vietnam War and performed many horrific acts on his enemies, as well as innocent women he had raped and killed.

Miguel showed the child many Polaroids of his exploits, and regularly beat his wife, Jessie, in front of Richard. This all came to a terrible climax on the night of May 4, 1973, when Mike went too far and fatally shot Jessie in the face with a revolver after an argument. Richard was left traumatized by the event and became withdrawn, eventually moving in with his sister Ruth and her husband. This is where he also began to venture into the consumption of LSD and dabbling in Satanism; a theme which would follow him until he was death. He had urgently needed to create some distance from home — Julian was heartbroken to see what his son was becoming, and before Richard left, they had been fighting practically all the time.

Miguel had not only taught him how to take drugs, but also how to kill animals stealthily and effectively. Richard was reunited with his veteran cousin only four years after his initial incarceration — he had been found not guilty by reason of insanity — and the older man's influence continued to spread. They went out on hunts and killed farm animals, with Richard soon learning how to gut a dead animal corpse.

Richard was a bad student, who had never interested in any subjects except for physical education, and he preferred to spend his time at video arcades, and reading about Satan and the fallen angels at the school library than studying for his exams. He began to break into homes during his teenage years and was caught several times with marijuana on his person, eventually agreeing to being sentenced to community service on three years probation to avoid prison. He had a diet of fast food and a high intake of sugar, his teeth began to rot. He also suffered from a severe case of halitosis.

Miguel's influence hadn't just been murder; Richard began to meld his sexual fantasies with violence and regularly dreamed of bondage and rape. He found a job at the Holiday Inn while still at school, and took advantage of his passkey to rob patrons of their belongings while they slept. He also hid behind curtains while unsuspecting female guests undressed and left without them noticing a thing. At one point, Ramirez was caught attempting to rape a guest's wife and was beaten senseless, but the couple didn't bother to return to testify against him. He was fired, but didn't suffer any further punishment due to his age, 15-years-old at the time, and the fact that he convinced everybody the woman had lured him to the room for sex.

At the age of 22, having dropped out of school and ended his probation, he moved to California, where he would settle definitely.

## A Bloody New Chapter

Ramirez arrived in L.A. without much in terms of money, and lived off the sales of marijuana he had bought for cheap in El Paso. He spent the money surviving on junk food and sleeping at motels. He regularly stole cars, as well as all of the valuables within them, abandoning them within days to avoid police heat. His brother Ruben was briefly present in his life, another career criminal who was also involved in burglarizing homes.

Cocaine was gaining heavy popularity in the city during those days, and Richard soon became another victim to it, his addiction forcing him to burglarize more homes and sell more stolen items. In the summer of 1978, he bound a woman, who he often consumed drugs with, and raped her repeatedly. No punishment would come from it, but it certainly opened Richard's sexual appetite to levels he hadn't yet seen.

Alone in L.A., and with the desire for support from a higher power, his attraction towards Satanism soon became a fully-fledged devotion. He began to read about Anton LaVey, the founder of the Church of Satan in San Francisco, and dreamed of joining one of the rituals that took place within it, but eventually decided to continue practicing his religion alone. In his mind, Richard believed himself a true disciple of Satan, one that was protected from his fellow man by the darkness.

He began his spree on June 28, 1984, but there is an often-overlooked crime that took place just a couple of months before that. On April 10, 1984, two children, Mei Leung and her brother, went into their apartment building's basement to search for something the boy had lost. Richard Ramirez lived close by and must have caught sight of the children descending at one point, and soon followed them down to the darkness. It didn't take him long to encounter Mei in the darkness, who for some reason had been separated from her brother.

Richard pounced on her from the shadows, tearing her clothes off partially as he proceeded to rape and stab her almost to death. Mei Leung may have screamed and she may have struggled, but nobody came to her rescue. When Richard was done, he strangled her to death and moved to finish the ritual killing: he hung her from a water spigot above them by her blouse with her feet just a few inches above the ground, in a pose similar to Christ's crucifixion. It was a heinous crime, and investigators stated that it was a saddening sight to encounter when they were called in to the scene. Mayor Dianne Feinstein held a press conference a few days later; offering $10,000 to whoever could offer any information on the murder, but it wasn't until 2009 when Ramirez's DNA linked him to the murder. He wasn't charged with the crime due to the fact that he was already sitting on death row at the time. A second suspect's DNA was tied to the case in 2012, but there isn't enough evidence to charge him — a convicted felon not yet publicly identified at this moment in time.

Mei was Ramirez's first victim, but not the one that made him famous. No, he still had plenty of distress to cause yet.

Richard Ramirez was about to die — metaphorically — and the dreaded *Night Stalker* was about to be born.

## Birth of the Night Stalker

Ramirez's murder of the nine-year-old Mei Leung must have been the last thing to push him into a rebirth of his persona — after all; he'd had a very atypical childhood marred with the seeds of violence implanted into him by his psychopathic uncle. He'd only needed to truly act out on them and begin his transformation into the monster he'd become.

Whether it's a coincidence or a cruel twist of fate for his victims, Richard was a massive fan of the rock band *AC/DC,* and he always enjoyed listening to the song *Night Prowler,* which is about a creature of the darkness who comes out to hunt at night. He would something similar to the creature in the song from June 28, 1984 forward; when he began his Night Stalker killing spree.

That night, Richard had been consuming cocaine and stepped out of the house in an altered state — he felt the desperate urge to defile and murder somebody, *anybody*.

It had been a hot, humid day in Los Angeles on that particular afternoon, and come evening it finally seemed like the climate was cooling a little. A 79-year-old woman named Jennie Vincow decided to take advantage of that fact and left her window open to let in the soft breeze which was making the night so pleasant and cool. It would be her biggest mistake; it would also be her last.

Gloved hands removed the window's mesh screen and opened it wider. Without making a single sound, he managed to gain access and immediately began to look around curiously, searching for any valuable that he could take with him. Drawers were searched and objects were overturned, but there was nothing he could trade for drugs or sex. This infuriated him, and he eventually came across Vincow's sleeping form. There was still something he could take, something he had wanted to take from the beginning. Her life.

Jennie barely had the chance to scream as Richard plunged the knife into her chest, struggling to push her attacker off her. With a feeling of pleasure and release, he stabbed her several more times in the chest, and finally placed a hand over her mouth and slashed her throat from ear to ear. The cut was so deep; it almost decapitated the unfortunate victim. As she laid dead, a pool of blood spreading across her, Richard stabbed her three more times for good measure and left through the same window he'd entered. He'd left some careless fingerprints behind after removing his gloves, but it wouldn't be enough for him to get caught. Not yet, at least.

Jennie's son, Jack, who lived in the same building and regularly visited his mother, found her corpse and immediately rushed to call the police. They had little to work on besides the fingerprints, and even they were nothing if no suspects with prints matching them were found. Ramirez would continue to murder as freely as he wished.

And he did.

Almost a year passed before he killed again, but this time he went out with a single purpose — to destroy the lives of several people.

It was the evening of March 17, 1985, and 22-year-old Maria Hernandez was driving her car into the parking garage of a Rosemead condominium. She lived comfortably with her roommate, 35-year-old Dayle Okazaki, and would never have imagined what would follow within moments. As she descended from her vehicle and pushed the button to shut the garage door and turn the lights off, a tall, unkempt man began to walk towards her with a .22-caliber revolver. Maria screamed and begged him to leave her alone, but the lights went out and the sound of a gunshot followed.

Maria was incredibly lucky, for her reflexive act of raising her hand to her face caused her keys to deflect the bullet that had flown straight towards her face. She was knocked to the ground, still alive, and Ramirez unknowingly stood over her and took her keys to enter the home and finish off the other woman he'd seen peeking through the window. Dayle hid behind the counter, hoping that she would be missed by the killer, and eventually she stopped hearing the man's footsteps. In an act of innocent foolishness, she lifted her head up over the counter again, but Richard was standing nearby. He shot her through the forehead, killing her instantly, and made his way out of the home.

Maria watched as he escaped, and Richard realized that she was alive. He pointed his gun at her once more, but something made him decide to spare her and he ran back to his car and left. All Maria could do was uselessly attempt to revive her roommate and friend before calling the police, her life now transformed forever.

Richard, meanwhile, was already looking for his next victim. He wouldn't even allow the night to pass before he moved on to his next kill. He was in a frenzy and only wanted to spill blood; it was all that he desired at the time and the only thing that could satisfy him after his previous crime. A Taiwanese-born woman named Tsia-Lian Yu was driving a yellow Chevrolet down a road when Ramirez decided to follow her for a few miles.

She would become his next victim in a ruthless murder — Richard soon grew tired of tailing her and rammed his stolen vehicle into hers, the woman's car lifting up off the pavement and then coming to a screeching halt. He forced his way into the car and dragged the dizzy Tsia-Lian out, screaming insults at her before firing his gun at her at point blank range and leaving her to die soon after.

Witnesses saw him, but he couldn't give a damn. After all, a bit of notoriety was just what he was looking for. It wouldn't be long before he got his first nickname: *The Valley Intruder.*

It would only be ten more days before he performed another cruel, violent killing in the area, his next victims an elderly couple in Whittier, California. Richard would kick his violent methods up a notch, his thirst for blood only getting worse as he killed. This particular double murder would take place on March 27, 1985, when Richard broke into a home at 2 a.m. with a gun in hand and shot 64-year-old Italian immigrant Vicente Zazzara in the head, killing him instantly. Even though Vicente's murder had been ugly, it would be his terrified wife, 44-year-old Maxine, who suffered the worst part of it. She awoke to the noise of the gunshot and stepped out of her room to see what was going on, but Ramirez was quick to assault her and bind her hands, aggressively beating her as he demanded to know the location of her valuables.

While Richard ransacked the room and found nothing, Maxine managed to escape the bonds and grabbed a shotgun from under the bed, but it wasn't loaded. Ramirez rapidly shot her three times with his handgun before searching for a carving knife from the kitchen. With it, he would mutilate her with several deep wounds; slicing apart her abdomen, neck, breasts, vagina, and face, and finally gouged out her eyes, which he placed in a jewelry box and kept as a souvenir. In a worrying discovery, the empty sockets were left with blackened blood and tissue within them, and not much else. As he walked outside, he left clear footprints in the household's flower bed, as well as bullet casings within the home, evidence which would be used against him in the future. In a curious twist, the couple's son would find their corpses, similarly to Jennie Vincow's murder.

On the 15th of May, 1985, Ramirez entered the home of another elderly couple — Bill Doi, 66, and the disabled Lillian, 56, both of Japanese descent — and came across Bill, who reached for his handgun to protect his home before the armed stranger could threaten him. He was too slow, and Ramirez shot him in the face before he could even lay his hands on the firearm. Richard knocked Bill out as his life bled out of him and proceeded to the next room, where Lillian lay terrified.

*"Shut up bitch, or I'll kill you,"* he growled, before handcuffing her and ransacking the home, but the ordeal wasn't over for Lillian yet. Richard tore her clothes

off and raped her. He soon left, and in a sad but heroic twist to the tale, Bill regained consciousness long enough to drag himself to Lillian's room and call the police. He would be dead within a few hours.

Again, Richard had left footprints behind, as well as fingerprints. These were recorded by police, but not enough action was taken beyond that to stop the serial killer who was brutalizing his victims.

Ramirez would strike two weeks later on May 29th in the town of Monrovia, northeast of Los Angeles, when he randomly selected the house of eighty-three-year-old Mabel Bell for his next rampage. Her 81-year-old disabled sister, Nettie Lang, also lived with her. They didn't lock their doors, for nobody in the area had seen the type of savage crimes that those within the City of Angels did. He would only need to push open her front door to enter the home.

Once within the house, Richard picked up a hammer in the kitchen and smashed Nettie's head repeatedly with it. Mabel received the same treatment, the hammer cracking her skull open like a watermelon and spraying blood and brains across the room. He then tore open an electrical cord and stabbed it into Mabel's body to shock her before also raping her. As he decided to leave, he spotted Lang's lipstick, which he used to draw a pentagram on her thigh and one on each of the rooms' walls.

The worst part of this horrific, inhuman double murder? *They were both still alive when he left and would take a few more days to die in excruciating pain.*

He drove to Burbank the very next day and sneaked into 42-year-old Carol Kyle's home. He had come across a locked front door at first, but used the dog flap in the back door to reach up and unlock his way inside the home. Carol never heard him until it was too late. He pointed a flashlight into her groggy eyes and warned her not to scream before asking who else was in the house. Kyle revealed that her 11-year-old son was in the next room, and Richard knew he could make things even more entertaining for himself. He asked Carol to lead him to the bedroom and she did so — reluctantly, but a gun to her head made refusing him difficult — Richard immediately opened the door and put his gun to his head. Carol begged him to leave him alone, and Richard accepted, placing the child inside the closet before raping the mother and sodomizing her with violence. He threatened to carve her eyes out if she struggled, so she withstood the horrible ordeal with bravery for her son;

Richard would finally leave after taking the boy out of the closet, handcuffing him to his half-naked mother's wrist and warning them that he would return with his friends if they reported the crime.

Richard killed again on June 27th, when he took the life of 28-year-old school teacher Patty Higgins in a savage attack, where he sodomized and nearly decapitated her in his rush to take her life through stabs and slashes to her neck.

On July 2, 1985, Richard drove nearby to 75-year-old Mary Louise Cannon's home in Arcadia, where he found her asleep in her room. He picked up a lamp on her dresser and used it to bludgeon her into unconsciousness, proceeding then to stab her in the throat a dozen times before ransacking the home and leaving quietly.

By this time, his nickname *The Valley Intruder* had long become too meek for the crimes he committed, and the media began to call him *The Night Stalker.* This moniker would remain with him until his death, and he was greatly proud of it.

# The Stalker's Savagery Increases

His next attack would take place on July 5, 1985, when he broke into a home and savagely bludgeoned a 16-year-old named Whitney Bennett with a tire iron while she slept. Having no luck in finding a knife in her kitchen to finish her off, the killer used a telephone cord to strangle her, but something happened. The cord tore apart and sparks flew out, and Richard flinched in fear. In his mind, Jesus Christ himself had saved the girl, so he escaped without stealing anything or hurting anybody else. Whitney survived, requiring 478 stitches to seal the lacerations on her scalp.

Two days later, he murdered Joyce Lucille Nelson, 61. He found her asleep in her room and beat her to death with his own fists and feet. He even left a shoe print on her face after he repeatedly stamped on it with his foot. It was the *same* Avia shoe print that he'd left in all of the other crime scenes, and police also had a pretty good physical description of the killer that was brutalizing so many people in the area.

Sophie Dickman, 63, was next that same night. She wasn't murdered, but he unsuccessfully attempted to rape her and stole her jewelry. He told her to swear on Satan that she wasn't hiding anything else and left after she did, handcuffing her to the bed before he disappeared into the night. Funnily enough, we could call her one of the *'lucky'* ones.

He went out to murder again on July 20, 1985, purchasing a machete before his next crime took place. Arriving at the home of Maxon, 68, and Lela Kneiding, 66, in the middle of the night, he entered their bedroom and kicked their bed after turning on the lights and screaming *"Rise and shine, bitches!"* When they awoke, terrified, Richard slashed down on Maxon's neck. He lost his grip on the machete before he could do the same to Lela and decided to shoot her, but the gun jammed. Eventually it fired, and he killed them both — despite Lela's begging — before robbing them of their valuables and mutilating their corpses.

Before the night was done, he drove to Chainarong and Somkid Khovananth's household, where he broke in and shot the sleeping Chainarong in the head with his handgun before repeatedly raping Somkid and forcing her to perform oral sex on him. The 8-year-old son of the couple was present during the entire ordeal. He and his mother would survive the attack, as well as another child. Somkid would help give the police valuable information that would help put Ramirez into custody.

Richard would murder again on both August 6 and August 8, claiming the life of a man named Elyas Abowath, raping his wife Sakina Abowath and leaving a couple, Chris and Virginia Peterson, injured; after using defective bullets which failed to kill them but left Virginia half-blind and mute, but the noose was closing on him after his face began to appear everywhere. He still believed that Satan was protecting him and always asked his victims to *swear to Satan* and not to God when he told them not to lie, but he knew that he still had to keep himself from getting caught nevertheless.

This brought him to the conclusion that he needed to find a new killing ground, a place where he could continue his work in a more discreet and concealed manner and where there were more serial killers, who he could hide behind as he took lives. This took him to Los Angeles, where he lasted only a few days without murdering.

On August 18, 1985, he took his next life; a 66-year-old man named Peter Pan, who he gunned down before raping Barbara, the man's 62-year-old wife. He shot her in the head and left her for dead before painting a pentagram on the wall with the words *"Jack the Knife"* beside it. Barbara would never walk again.

Terror hit the city of San Francisco when detectives revealed that the bullet which had killed Pan had indeed came from the *Night Stalker's* gun, and Mayor Dianne Feinstein appeared in a televised press conference. In her ignorance, she regrettably revealed that police were following a killer who was leaving his shoeprints behind at many scenes. Richard was indeed watching the conference and discarded his shoes that very night, setting back the investigation thanks to his unexpected ally.

Even so, it would be his two next crimes which finally decided his fate.

On August 24, 1985, he traveled to Mission Viejo, 76 miles south of L.A., where he arrived at the home of James Romero Jr., whose 13-year-old son was still awake despite the late hour. Ramirez approached the house, but the teen heard him and ran outside to see what was going on. Richard escaped, but James was able to make out the details and license plate of the car, which he offered to the police a few moments later in a phone call. The killer had also left a footprint behind.

That same night, Richard broke into the home of Bill Carns and Inez Erickson. He shot the former in the head twice, and both raped and sodomized the latter, but didn't kill her. Not only did she heroically withstand the ordeal to help her husband to a neighbor's house quick enough for him to survive despite the two bullets lodged in his head, but she also gave the police very valuable information which — along with Romero's own details of the stolen car which Richard was driving — led them to find the vehicle on August 28 in Los Angeles. There was a fingerprint on its rearview mirror. After testing, police finally made a match.

The fingerprint belonged to a 25-year-old Richard Muñoz Ramirez, a repeat offender who had arrests for traffic and illegal drugs. His mug shot was released, and an announcement was made:

*"We know who you are now, and soon everyone else will. There will be no place you can hide."*

Ironically enough, the Night Stalker was about to walk out into the daylight in a foolish twist of events. *It would be his downfall.*

## The Final Conclusion

On August 30, Ramirez metaphorically toppled the first domino piece which would lead to his capture. He had decided to visit his brother in Tucson, Arizona, but chose the worst time of day to do so; in broad daylight. He was a wanted man, his face known to everyone, and ultimately it was an act of stupidity on his part.

After returning without having seen his brother, he left the Los Angeles station without issues, despite a number of police watching the place in hopes of catching him, and arrived at a convenience store. It only took an instant for some elderly Mexican women to spot him and cry out, *"It's him, the asesino; killer!"*

Richard fled as more and more people got involved, and saw his face on the newspapers he passed. He ran for two miles, with an increasing number of people pointing at him and crying out his name. *"Night Stalker, Night Stalker!"* It led him to attempt to carjack a woman, but he was chased away. Encountering another car — with its owner, Faustino Pinon working under it — he tried to escape inside it, but Pinon grabbed on him and swatted Richard's handgun away to the ground as he produced it from his pocket. Richard managed to ignite the engine and drove away, but Pinon was still grabbing at him, causing the killer to crash in to a garage door. Richard got out of the vehicle and the two struggled, but the Night Stalker knew he had to run before it was too late.

His very last attempt at escaping took him to Angelina Torres, a 28-year-old who was driving down the street in a Ford Granada. Richard threw half his body through the driver's window and threatened to kill her if she didn't hand over the keys and vehicle, but her husband heard her screams and began to beat the killer with a metal rod, with family members and neighbors joining in. He managed to get a few steps away before he was outnumbered and subdued. The blows rained down on him as the police arrived and took him away.

*Finally,* after fourteen murders and eleven rapes, it could be said that the deadly Night Stalker was in custody.

On September 20, 1989, Ramirez was convicted with 13 counts of murder, 5 attempted murders, 11 sexual assaults and 14 burglaries. He was sentenced to die in a gas chamber, and everyone was relieved.

It wouldn't matter, though…

...he died in 2013 from B-cell lymphoma, after having spent 23 years imprisoned and waiting for his execution.

Richard Ramirez was a true bastard. Even during his trial, he showed up with a pentagram painted on his hand, mocked the victims, and posed for dozens of pictures that were taken for documentation.

One of the members of the jury was murdered before a session took place, but it was concluded that it had been her boyfriend, who also committed suicide.

Ramirez did not pass through the world without leaving his mark — you either loved him or you hated him, and he had a very large cult following that wanted either to meet him or have sex with him, or both. He even got married with one of the many women who exchanged letters with him for years.

Richard was no common killer; he was one of the most controversial, unique, and absolutely fucked-up human beings you will ever hear about.

Whether it is in hatred or in regret, the Night Stalker shall be remembered...*forever.*

# FIVE

-----------------------------

## The Highway Stalker

**W**e've already seen how dangerous a killer can be when he has a like-minded accomplice at his side who can serve him in his heinous acts, but what about when you have a fully-fledged serial killer working alongside another one? Two men who have joined forces — and formed a homosexual relationship, as well — to start a rampage across the United States and tear apart the lives of so many people that they eventually lost count of the true number of victims? It sounds like the worst nightmare you could ever have.

Yet it happened — **Henry Lee Lucas**, our next killer, and **Ottis Toole**, a man known as *The Jacksonville Cannibal,* became friends, lovers, and tag-team killers. They roamed along the highways of Texas and Virginia in search of vulnerable victims such as hitchhikers, who they would abuse and murder with a sick pleasure that was born of their need to cause pain and despair.

This story is not a pretty one, for Henry's violence was born from violence: the hatred and abuse received from his mother, a true witch of a woman who served to create a despicable serial killer who would go on to kill between 3 and 3000 people.

This is the story of the *Confession Killer* and his best friend, two men who, after traumatic childhoods that no other man or woman would envy, became two of the worst criminals in American history.

## Corrupted At Birth

Henry Lee Lucas never stood a chance. He was born into a household of sexual deviancy and violence, and to be fair to him, it was always going to end badly.

It was on August 23, 1936, when Viola Lucas gave birth to Henry in Blacksburg, Virginia, in a rural community within the Appalachian Trail. The family was extremely poor and dysfunctional — Viola was an abusive, troubled woman dedicated to prostitution and alcohol, who had had nine children when Henry came along; Anderson "No Legs" Lucas was an alcoholic who had lost his lower extremities many years before in an unfortunate railroad accident.

Viola cared little for her children or husband, even going as far as attending her clients within the home in front of them. There wasn't much of a choice for the family either — they lived in a cramped, one-room log cabin which didn't allow much in terms of privacy. Viola violently abused the rest of her family when she drank too much, which was often, and she neglected the necessities that her kids had, which were many.

She tormented Henry by dressing him as a girl, cutting his hair into feminine ringlets and sent him to school barefoot on many occasions. On one particular incident, a teacher gifted him with a teddy bear to lift his spirits, but Viola beat him bloody for it. On another occasion, a friend of Anderson's gifted Henry with a mule, and his mother loaded a gun and fatally shot the animal for no reason whatsoever.

When Henry was just t8-years-old, Viola hit him with a wooden plank during one of her fits of rage. She hit him so hard that the boy was left in a coma that lasted three days, ending only when one of his mother's lovers, *"Uncle Bernie"* took him to a hospital where he was given medical assistance. Henry's siblings weren't exactly normal either: although many of them had been given away to adoption or left the home, his older half-brother was another negative influence on Henry's life and would eventually introduce the boy to bestiality, killing said animals once they were done abusing them. This same brother also cut Henry's eyelid open with a knife during a fight, and the child would only be taken to see a doctor when the wound had grown heavily infected. This caused Henry to lose his eye; it would be replaced with a glass eye and his eyelid would droop over it for the rest of his life.

Henry's parents owned a still, where they brewed moonshine whiskey; Anderson regularly allowed his youngest son to drink the product, causing Henry to become an alcoholic at the tender of age of 10.

Anderson was as much Viola's victim as Henry was, and he regularly drank booze to attempt to get over the depression of his medical condition, the poverty they were going through and the fact that his wife disrespected him with a constant stream of lovers coming in and out of his home; unfortunately, one day it became too much. Anderson went outside during a blizzard after having drunk more than usual and didn't come back. His body was found later — he'd died of pneumonia, but clearly he'd been seeking to end it all.

Soon after, while Henry was in sixth grade, he ran away. The boy knew that now with Anderson gone, he'd be the sole target of his mother's abuse. He drifted around Virginia, where he would later state that he committed his first murder at the age of 15; a 17-year-old who Henry abducted from a bus stop before beating unconscious and raping. He confessed to having strangled her after the rape, but would later retract this statement. Even so, a girl matching his description named Laura Burnsley was killed in similar circumstances around the date he gave in his recount.

Even so, whether or not the murder took place or not, Henry was already warming up for something deadly.

## Getting Even

Having learned nothing of value during his childhood and early teenage years, Henry soon became a burglar who attacked at least a dozen homes in the Richmond area along with at least two of his half-brothers before he was arrested and sentenced to four years in prison.

On September 14, 1957, he managed to escape and attempted to head to his sister's home but was recaptured; he would eventually be released on September 2, 1959. He had already spent a short time in the Beaumont training school for boys a few years before.

Henry had a sister named Opal in Tecumseh, Michigan. She always asked him to come and live with her so that he could turn things around, and after prison he decided to accept. After all, he would be far away from his mother and everything he had done in Virginia. He had also met and fallen in love with a girl named Stella, and they planned to marry.

Unfortunately, things wouldn't be so easy. His mother, now older, was of a different opinion. She visited her son and his new fiancée and told him what she believed he had to do: Henry had to leave Stella and stay at home to help her out more than ever now that she was weaker and less able than before. Henry refused and a violent argument followed, one which spooked Stella and made the young woman leave him for good. Henry was heartbroken and furious, and decided to go to Opal's home to cool off and have some drinks, but Viola followed him. She insisted that he return home with her, to the point where the argument started again.

This time, however, Henry had had enough of his mother and her orders. He kindly told her to go back to where she'd come from, and this drove Viola into a rage. She grabbed a broom and hit it across his head as she'd done so many times before; breaking it, but Henry wasn't a helpless little boy anymore. He threw himself on his mother and struck her in the neck with the first object he could grab and watched her fall to the ground. Only then did he realize that he'd cut open her throat with a knife.

He panicked and turned the lights off before running out of the apartment and driving back to Virginia, in fear of getting caught for killing his mother. Funnily enough, Viola would live for another two days, when Opal finally came back and found her mother bleeding out on the kitchen floor. The abusive woman didn't make it to the hospital, and the cause of death was stated as being the heart attack that followed the assault and not the wound itself.

Henry was arrested soon after in Ohio, where he claimed to have been already thinking of returning to Michigan to turn himself in. It didn't matter anyway: he was sent back to Michigan and tried in court for his crime. There, he claimed that he had killed his mother in self-defense, but the claim was rejected and he was sentenced to between 20 and 40 years for second degree murder in the State Prison of Southern Michigan.

## Career Criminal

Prison certainly made Henry Lee a worse person than the one he'd already been, and he began to openly complain of hearing incessant voices in his head — including his mother's, telling him to commit suicide for killing her. He was filled with suicidal thoughts and attempted to kill himself twice by slashing his wrists and stomach with a razor. Both times, jail staff stopped him and he was transferred to Iona State mental hospital in hopes of treating his condition with drugs and painful electro-shock therapy. Neither served their purpose: upon his transfer away from the hospital and back to the penitentiary, Henry asked not to be released because he was sure he'd kill again. His request was ignored.

To make matters worse, Lucas didn't even serve his whole sentence: overcrowding in the prison system turned him into a low-priority prisoner, and he was released just ten years into his sentence, in June 1970. He left the penitentiary with an ugly warning to the guards, *"I'll leave you a present on the way out,"* he snarled as they escorted him out; he'd later state that he'd killed two women within the sight of the prison, but this was never confirmed.

Henry was once again a free man, though it wouldn't last long. He fucked up again just a few months later, landing himself in jail for attempting to kidnap two teenage girls, and was sent back to the same prison for another five years. There, he would begin a relationship with an old family friend and single mother, Betty Crawford.

After his release, Lucas married the woman, but it wouldn't last — she soon found out he was sexually abusing her step-daughters and divorced him. He returned to his drifter days, his travels taking him across several states. His later confessions would tell of how he murdered many during these years, but no evidence has been found of such. He got a job in West Virginia and visited Louisiana and West Virginia, but finally his travels took him all the way to Jacksonville, Florida, where the impoverished, homeless man decided to find a mission that provided free food and shelter.

There, he would meet his best friend, lover, accomplice, and fellow killer, **Ottis Toole**.

Ottis was a man who had also been a victim of sexual assault as a child, the son of two abusive alcoholics — his mother had dressed him as a girl and his father had been absent, just like Henry — and the result had been similar; they had succeeded in creating a deranged killer.

The homosexual Toole didn't take long to feel charmed by Lucas, who, like him, had suffered a traumatic childhood and was regularly invaded with murderous thoughts. The two shared their exploits with each other, and finally Ottis invited his new buddy to his family's home.

There, Lucas grew attached to Toole's teenage niece, Frieda 'Becky' Powell, who along of suffering from a mild mental condition, was already promiscuous at the age of eleven. He began living with the girl, working as a roofer and fixing cars to provide them with a sort of stability. This continued until 1981, when Ottis Toole's mother died, and the trio of Toole, Lucas, and Powell began to travel around the interstate highways. Accounts are conflicting around these years, as both killers would later confess to have joined a cannibalistic murder cult named, *"The Hands of Death,"* for whom they murdered up to 108 people together.

Ottis was said to have inducted Lucas into the cult, with the latter even having to slice a man's throat open as a test of initiation. Hitchhikers, people with broken-down vehicles, prostitutes, and travelers were all targeted by the pair. One of their victims was believed to be found naked in a field with thirty-five stab wounds and deep cuts on the cold, dead body.

Whatever truly happened in this bloody period, it ended with at least two confirmed murders that finally put the murderer behind bars for good.

## Kate and Becky

Lucas eventually separated from Ottis Toole after a disagreement, and the former took Becky with him on more aimless travels until they reached Texas in 1982. Again, looking for a change of scenery, Henry began to work for an elderly woman named Kate Rich, who lived in the small farming town of Ringgold. He and Becky assisted the old woman on her ranch, but also began to take advantage of her trust and stole from her.

It wasn't until the old woman's family members realized that the two new arrivals were not only charging work they never performed, but also cashing checks on her bank account that Lucas and Powell were kicked out of Rich's home and back onto the streets once more. This made Henry bitter and angry, but he accepted to keep looking for a place he could establish himself in.

The couple continued their travels and soon found themselves in Stoneburg, Texas, where a friendly minister, Ruben Moore, invited them to join a religious commune named, *"The House of Prayer."* He trusted Henry Lee and Becky as the unfortunate married couple they appeared to be, and offered Henry work as a roofer within the community. Things worked for a few months, but Becky soon grew homesick and tired of the commune. She didn't want to be there anymore, and she asked Lucas if they could return home.

What went through Lucas' mind then was a mystery, but what *is* known is that he took Becky away from the commune and all the way up to a lonely field in Denton County so that they could spend the night. Becky continued to ask Lucas if they could return, and the man was emphatic in telling her that they couldn't. One thing led to another and Powell made the mistake of slapping him in the head during an argument. Henry, not for the first time, saw red. He didn't hesitate to ram a knife into Powell's chest, killing her almost immediately. He had sex with her body after she was dead, and claimed to have enjoyed it. Realizing that he had to dispose of the corpse, he dismembered it with the same knife and scattered its parts around the field.

He returned to the ranch of Kate Rich, claiming with tears in his eyes that Becky had gotten into a passing truck and left him for good. Kate was inquisitive, showing clear signs of distrust in his version of the tale. Her suspicion eventually became so blatant that Henry felt threatened and decided to murder her. He stabbed the old woman and carved an inverted cross on her chest before having sex with her dead body. He then threw her body into a ditch, but days later would return to cut the body up and separate it into garbage bags, stuffing them all inside a drainage pipe.

With both Becky and Kate dead, he now knew he had to keep moving and avoid any suspicious behavior if he truly desired to continue his time as a free man. Police began to suspect Henry of being involved in the murder of Kate Rich due to his previous issues with her, and he was brought in for a polygraph test. Through some unknown means which manipulated his reactions to the questions asked, Henry managed to pass the test without raising any alarms. His car was searched and blood was found, but it didn't match Rich's; results revealed that it was Henry's own.

Henry would soon escape and continue his travels, but the authorities were about to catch up to him.

Funny thing is, he was ultimately the reason for his own downfall...

## Between Truths and Falsehoods

Lucas was arrested in Texas by Texas Ranger Phil Ryan on charges of unlawful possession of a firearm. He was kept in a cold cell and reported to have been mistreated by fellow inmates. The thing is, authorities had a bad feeling about the man they just couldn't shake, and among them there was a belief that giving the man a bit of discomfort would work in easing the truth out of him.

It certainly *did* work; four days later, Henry called over his jailer and told him he wanted to talk about the *'bad things'* he'd been doing. Confession investigators came to the jail and heard what he had to say.

*"To Whom It May Concern, I, Henry Lee Lucas, to try to clear this matter up, I killed Kate Rich on September last year. I have tried to get help so long and*

*no one will help. I have killed for the past 10 years and no one will believe it."*

Lucas' belief was that if the police wanted to pin a murder he *hadn't* done on him, he would have to tell them of all the ones he *had*. His first confessions were the only murders that were corroborated by evidence — Rich and Powell — but went on to confess dozens, then hundreds, and finally thousands of murders which were mostly a mix of exaggerated facts and downright lies that Lucas made up to keep himself important to the police in the case; they were even allowing him to regularly dine out of the prison and walk around with his hands uncuffed, leading several experts to decide how to manage the matter.

Among those who worked to discredit the killer was a female detective by the name of Linda Erwin who meticulously fabricated a murder and asked Lucas about it; he quickly confessed to having been behind it, giving details in a way that would have been credible in court. On another occasion, a Ranger asked him if he'd ever killed anyone in Guyana, and the killer nodded. Apparently, Henry had driven his car there himself. The mixed truths made the case a mess, especially because he *had* killed more than two people, it was just a matter of separating the truth from the lies.

Finally, this led to the creation of *"The Lucas Report,"* a study that helped determine the murderous timeline and Henry's known locations as each murder took place. With it, detectives managed to glean the truth from the dirt. Henry was convicted for eleven murders, though continued to be suspected in the murder of many more, and he was sentenced to death. This sentence was commuted by Governor George W. Bush, *sound familiar,* to life in prison in 1998, due to confirmation that Henry had not been behind the murder of an unidentified woman known only as *'Orange Socks,'* for the way she was found naked and wearing only those garments.

Henry didn't get to live his life in prison, however. He was found dead in March, 2001, at the age of 64; his heart had given out. Strangely enough, his buddy Ottis had a similar end; his death sentence had been commuted to six consecutive life sentences, but cirrhosis took him in 1996.

Henry Lee Lucas' death closed the doors on many murders and some were hastily marked as *'solved'* after his confessions, but the truth is that we still cannot truly

123

tell how many people Henry Lee Lucas murdered, and if, perhaps, there are many other serial killers roaming freely after he covered their back with his confessions.

As recently as 2015, there have been discoveries on possible victims which Henry confessed to murdering, and it may be that Lucas is one of the serial killers law enforcement *didn't* want to see dead, especially with everything that he may have taken with him to his grave.

Even after his death, Henry has us guessing — was he the most prolific serial killer in America? Or was he just the best liar?

We may never know.

# SIX

------------------------------

## The Killer Nurse

We've reached our final killer, and this one is quite different from the ones before her.

Our following murderer was a woman who didn't end the lives of her victims — infants, in their majority — because she enjoyed killing, but because she had a need in her life to be seen as a heroine that could work miracles on the kids that she treated. Family deaths had torn her mind apart, and she felt the need to save lives at any cost, even if it meant putting children in danger. She was a nurse at a children's hospital with plenty of jurisdiction, and it was like putting a wolf among sheep.

**Genene Anne Jones,** our final murderer, managed to kill again and again, and her records seemed to be wiped clean every time she was about to get into trouble, leading her to murder at least eleven children and damage the health and well-being of dozens more.

We shall begin her tale, the tale of this *Angel of Death*, and with it end this blood-soaked list of murderers…

## A Girl Misled by Pain

Genene Anne Jones was born on July 13, 1950, to unknown parents who immediately set her up for adoption. She was given a home by Richard "Dick" and Gladys Jones, who would also go on to adopt three other kids. The family was wealthy and they lived comfortably in a two-story, four bedroom mansion outside the city of San Antonio. Dick was an entrepreneur and gambler, and his first business as a father was a nightclub at their home; the Kit Kat Swim Club, which he managed and acted as host while his wife spun records on the turntable. He was a tall and imposing but also generous man with ambitious plans in life, and a loving father.

When the nightclub failed, Dick tried again with a restaurant, but it went down a similar road. He was of the free-spending kind, not a man to save money for hard times. He was arrested when Genene was just ten years old; having been involved in stealing a man's safe from his home and storing it in his club. There was $1,500 in cash and some jewelry within, and Dick was held by the police until he confessed it was just a practical joke, which had been played on the victim. The charges were dropped.

Soon, he began a billboard business, and that's where Genene comes into the story. She was a hard worker at his company, even as a child. She helped him paint and put up the billboards across town, and recalled it as the happiest period of her life. Unfortunately, young Genene constantly needed attention, to the point where she always felt left out, ignored and unloved by her parents no matter what they did. She considered herself the family's "black sheep." To find her much-needed attention, she often pretended to be sick or exaggerated her problems, as well as bossing around her classmates in school. She wasn't a pretty or thin girl either, and this didn't help her self-esteem.

Genene's best friend was her brother Travis, who would spend time with her and her dad at the billboard shop. Unfortunately, Travis died in a careless accident, when a pipe bomb he'd constructed blew up in his face and killed him instantly. She was 16 when it happened, and is said to have never been the same afterwards. Further trauma followed a year later when Dick was diagnosed with terminal cancer, his mind already made up on the sad decision of not taking treatment. The 57-year-old barely put up a fight against his illness and lasted only a few months.

Both deaths hit Genene a bit too hard, and she was devastated by the news. Her mother Gladys, too, was left distraught and soon began to drink heavily. Genene felt lonelier than ever. In her mind there was a simple solution to her solitude; to find someone to get married with. Gladys didn't agree and refused to give her permission, but Genene did so regardless; she married a high school dropout by the name of Jimmy Harvey Delaney as soon as she graduated at the age of 18, having coerced him into doing so by making him believe she was pregnant.

The marriage was a dysfunctional one. The couple didn't really love each other, and as soon as Jimmy enlisted in the navy, Genene began to sleep with other men and boast about it. She made up stories about her childhood, such as being the victim of rape, and began affairs with multiple married men. She didn't even work — her mother had to provide for her, and Gladys was finally forced to talk her daughter into finding a job.

Genene enrolled at Mim's Beauty School and became a beautician. She took a job at the Method Hospital Beauty Parlor and began to file papers for divorce, stating that her husband had been abusive and often struck her with brutality. Despite this, when Harvey returned, she still managed to have a child with him in 1972, while the divorce was underway. When she won a court order barring her husband from her and her baby son, Richard Michael Delaney, something made her reconcile with her husband, causing the judge to dismiss the suit.

The couple split up once again in 1974, and this time it was permanent. She had another child, a girl, who she called Heather. She swore in a legal document that the girl was the daughter of another man, but would later confess to a co-worker that Heather was also Jimmy's. Around this time, tragedy struck her life again — her older brother passed to cancer, bringing the pain rushing back to her all over again. Genene made a decision. She didn't want to watch anyone else die; she wanted to save lives.

She wanted to be a nurse.

# Paved With Good Intentions

Genene left her children in the care of her mother and began her plan. Working at a hospital beauty salon had been a platform for her to involve herself in the field of health. All she needed now was to find a way to become a vocational nurse, so she did. Her dream was to be a doctor, but if she could start off as a nurse, she'd be content. Her training at the San Antonio Independent School District's School of Vocational Nursing took her a year to complete — she was an excellent student with mostly 90's in her grades. Immediately, she was offered a job at the Methodist Hospital, though only eight months later, in April 1978, she was asked to leave. According to Genene, she had a conflict with a doctor's diagnosis and argued with him in front of the patient. They asked her to resign immediately after. This would become a recurring theme; Genene would rarely accept that she was wrong, even when a patient's life depended on it.

Her next job was in the obstetrics-gynecology ward at Community Hospital. There, she had to resign to undergo minor surgery, and when she was back on her feet decided to send her resume to Bexar County Hospital, where she was assigned to work in the pediatric intensive care unit on October 30, 1978.

The story truly begins there.

Genene would come to claim that she was terrified on her first day in Bexar County, picking up a baby with a case of necrotizing enterocolitis and immediately realizing she had found her calling. A registered nurse, Cherlyn Pendergraft, who gave Jones her orientation would counter these comments and claim that Genene behaved extremely strangely when the boy returned to the ICU and succumbed to his illness. Pendergraft spoke about how Genene went insane when the boy died; collapsing on a stool at the dead baby's side and crying in deep, wracking sobs. She and other nurses found it hard to understand, after all, Genene had only been around him for hours at best.

Other, more experienced nurses immediately began to spot the strange behavior that Genene demonstrated: she spent long hours of her shift on the ward, watching patients for abnormally long periods and insisting that her presence was essential to their well-being. She had skipped classes on the handling of drugs and made several nursing mistakes. Even when said errors were pointed out to her, she sometimes ignored the

advice and did what she thought best for the children —
even when it *wasn't* the best. In her defense, she was very
inquisitive and spent a lot of time researching what she
didn't know in books, but experience would always trump
textbooks, and it didn't forgive the fact that she was
contradicting nurses who had been doing their thing for
years. She even went to work **drunk** on one occasion.

Unfortunately for her fellow nurses and the patients, the
head nurse, Pat Belko, liked and respected Genene, and
this meant that Jones was even more sure of herself and
her capabilities than she should have been. Belko even
defended Jones — and herself, to a point — after the
deaths became public, saying that Genene *"Understood a
lot of anatomy and physiology that was on a higher level
than a lot of LVNs;* Licensed Vocational Nurses. *For an
LVN, she was excellent."* This feeling towards her made
Genene feel like a genuine ICU nurse.

Genene didn't have bad intentions, that much is
for sure. She frequently volunteered to work over-time
and was a truly marvelous talent at introducing
intravenous lines into veins. She soon became the go-to
nurse for starting IV's, even in the smallest, most restless
patients. Many other nurses disliked her, but almost all of
them respected what she could do.

As her experience and respect from other nurses grew, Genene became more arrogant and foul-mouthed. She no longer cared about who was around when she began criticizing other nurses and doctors, and she often spoke about her sexual conquests with patients around to hear. She also made cold comments about dying children, predicting when she believed they would die.

Her propensity to make false diagnoses soon caused frictions between her and the resident doctors, who grew tired of her calls while they were attempting to rest after long hours on the ward. She spread her horrible, pessimistic predictions to anyone who would hear her, and regularly exaggerated to make it look as if stable patients were dying. Jones showed a completely different face to the parents of the children, however; to them, she was the friendliest, most caring nurse in the hospital.

Although things were already tense at Bexar County, the arrival of Doctor James Robotham made things worse. His approach was similar to Genene's, and he rapidly became her biggest ally. The doctor would show up at the hospital at the merest call; he'd create false crises for his nurses to solve; and regularly humiliated residents who couldn't answer his unexpected questions. His role was to take over as the ICU medical director and he did that job pretty well. *Too* well, some would argue, as his aggressive nature soon caused conflict and discomfort among both residents and nurses, who already had their own way of doing things; a way that worked.

Genene, meanwhile, was feeling over the moon that she had found someone who paid attention to her. Robotham appreciated the way she responded to situations; he saw her as an embodiment of what he needed in the ICU. Genene felt that finally she had found a doctor who had the patience to listen to her when she needed it.

At the time, Nurse Jones began to visit clinics during her free time, often complaining about her health and creating issues that neither she nor the attending doctors could prove existed. Some thought she had a form of Munchausen Syndrome; which causes people to act as if they have physical or mental disorders when they're actually fine, while another doctor claimed that she suffered from psychosomatic disorders.

The arrival of Doctor James Robotham allowed Jones to demand something she'd been asking for a while — to be put in charge of the sickest patients. She began to spend a lot of time around dying children, kids who she watched closely until they died. Once they had stopped breathing, Genene bathed them and took them to the morgue herself. On occasion, she was heard singing to a child after they had given their last breath, as well as weeping as she carried their bodies.

But nobody was asking *why* those children were dying. Nobody seemed to care, at first, *why* there were an increasing number of children perishing from typically non-fatal illnesses.

The truth was that Genene had already begun to do her damage...

## The Death Shift

During a single two-week period, seven children died in the ICU. This was a previously unseen occurrence, and even worse was the fact that now resuscitations were regularly being performed, an act which seldom had been needed before. Children were now going from being almost perfectly fine to suddenly flat-lining and needing immediate attention before they could lose their life.

The strange coincidence was that most of these events were taking place during Jones' shift. She was quick to joke about it as well, commenting on the fact that she was starting to look like the hospital's *"Death Nurse."* In truth, her fellow staff were calling her duty hours the *"3-11 Death Shift,"* a name that would stick when the events continued.

The first child to make the name even more fitting and truly raise alarms was six-month-old Jose Antonio Flores, who came in on October 10, 1981, with fever, vomiting, and diarrhea. They were treatable, common symptoms in an infant, but somehow when Genene stepped up to take care of him, he began to develop seizures and went into cardiac arrest. He was revived and brought back to the pediatric ICU. There, he began to bleed uncontrollably, and despite attempts to resuscitate him, his heart stopped beating. While the cause of death was reported as unknown, Genene Jones had been present while everything had taken place. The little boy's father had had a heart attack when he heard the news, and the family went to recover the body. For whatever reason going through her head at that moment, Genene grabbed the dead baby and ran to the morgue. Further suspicions rose when blood tests done on the child revealed a large amount of heparin — an anticoagulant — in the child's blood.

Another child named Albert Garza was found to have an overdose of heparin. He had also been treated by Jones, and she felt insulted when they asked her about it. More children began to develop bleeding issues, with blood leaking inexplicably from their mouths and rectums, eventually leading their blood pressure to drop and their hearts to suffer as a result. Robotham decided that heparin should be controlled more strictly, and the use of the substance began to require supervision. He also ordered that a review be made to investigate the deaths in the ICU.

Genene began to complain of medical ailments, regularly showing no evidence of being sick at all. Whenever she was offered drugs from worried doctors, she refused, and many began to think that she was simply looking for attention. Robotham no longer admired her as he had, and he began to air his complaints about the nurse.

Heparin was carefully watched, but the other drugs used were not. Another child died in mysterious circumstances: Joshua Sawyer, 11-months-old. He'd come in after inhaling smoke during a fire at his home and suffering cardiac arrest, but after being treated with Dilantin began to recover. Somehow and very unexpectedly, however, he had two heart attacks and died. Blood tests revealed an overdose of Dilantin, but nobody got in trouble for it.

Robotham's review was completed by January 1982. No sign of wrongdoing came from it, and the medical director relaxed. Unfortunately, the worst was yet to begin.

Four-week-old Rolando Santos had come to the hospital on December 27, 1981, the infant's pneumonia and breathing problems worrying his parents. Three days later, he began to have seizures, and a brain scan was unable to reveal any reasons why. He then suffered a cardiac arrest and was revived, and two days later, he began to bleed from the places where he'd been punctured with needles. He was urinating so much that he suffered from an extreme bout of dehydration. The doctor tending to the child decided to order tests that could indicate the presence of heparin. They came back positive. Whenever Genene was in charge of his care, the boy would worsen. Finally, the doctor had him removed from the ICU and placed under 24-hour surveillance; despite the fact that he normally would have been deemed too sick to be moved. Rolando soon got better, and the first true signs of foul play became obvious.

Heparin was removed from patients' bedside tables and a formal evaluation started. Genene was still not a true suspect, though some were whispering her name as the culprit.

Another baby, four-month-old Patrick Zavala, died from irregularities in his heartbeat after a simple operation, and this rocked both nurses and doctors. The latter were furious at what was happening to the patients they worked hard to save during their surgeries, and the director of the county hospital district got involved to keep things under control. Something had to be done.

Finally though, another doctor stepped forward and told the people in charge that Genene Jones was killing the children. He had found a manual among her possessions that spoke of ways to inject heparin without leaving a mark. Though the hospital didn't take immediate action, it helped put Genene in their sights. After yet another death and Genene's absurd reaction to it; squirting fluid over his forehead in the sign of a cross and over herself as well, Pat Belko and James Robotham decided to replace the LVNs on the unit with RNs;

registered nurses. A furious Genene decided to resign as a result, and hospital administration was relieved.

Unfortunately, in covering everything up and never directly charging her for what she'd done, they had only shifted the Genene problem to somebody else.

Things were only going to get worse.

## Dr. Holland's Mistake

Kathleen Mary Holland was a young, hungry doctor who had worked alongside Genene during her residency at Bexar County. She wanted to go into private practice in Kerrville, a town with the largest general hospital in the area but with a lack of pediatrics. To Kathleen, this was a challenge that she would promptly take care of.

She began to think of nurses who could help her — she spoke first to Pam Sturm, a registered nurse. Pam was delighted to hear the news, but rejected the offer. She was making too much for Holland to pay, but instead she suggested Kathleen look for an LVN. Eventually, Holland found the one she'd be searching for. *Genene Jones.* They'd worked together and the doctor respected her, often feeling impressed by the other woman's instinct to know when a child's health would worsen. Genene herself gave an initial 'no' to Holland, but the doctor was insistent.

Kathleen had already done her homework when she employed Genene; it could be that nobody was convincing enough for her not to employ the nurse. A doctor named Jolene Bean told Kathleen to change her mind, but Kathy didn't listen to her; however, neither Pat Belko nor James Robotham, who could have truly stopped the tragedy, were clear enough in telling her that they believed that Genene was killing babies.

The clinic opened on August 23, 1982. Genene's license had expired and she didn't renew it until November 29, meaning that she worked under Holland without a valid license; even so, things started well enough and Holland was happy.

Unfortunately, it didn't take long for the ugliness to begin. During a short period, seven different children began to suffer from seizures, and on one occasion, a fellow nurse saw her inject a child with something before an episode began. To make matters more suspicious, the children, who were always taken to hospital after the seizures began, would always recover and never have another episode again.

The first patient to die after being treated at the clinic was Chelsea McClellan. The child had been born premature and the delivery had been difficult, and her frail little body had evidence of a hyaline membrane disease — a common problem found in premature children. Even so, she was healthy at the time of her death on September 17, her parents long having learned how to take care of her when she lost her breath and fell unconscious. She died in a small hospital they'd headed to while on the way to Santa Rosa Hospital, the official autopsy blaming it on sudden infant death syndrome. Even so, Genene had tended to her and given her at least two shots in front of her mother. Each shot had made the child worse, but Chelsea's parents did not ultimately blame Genene. Instead, they thanked her for what had seemed to them was highly-professional care.

That very same day, another child was brought to the clinic, and he too suffered seizures. He had to be resuscitated. Meanwhile, at Sid Peterson Hospital a doctor discovered the high amount of deaths that had occurred while Genene Jones had been on her shift there. Kathleen was called in, and she was asked if she was using succinylcholine, a muscle relaxant. She nodded, adding that she didn't use it herself. When she left the Hospital, someone at the meeting informed the Texas Rangers. Genene Jones was now a prime suspect.

Dr. Holland returned to the clinic and informed Genene of the meeting. Genene quickly responded by telling her that she'd found a missing bottle of succinylcholine. Holland inspected it and the other available bottle while Genene was at lunch and found that they were both nearly full but had pinprick holes in their stoppers. Genene had no proper answer as to why. Dr. Holland later checked the bottles again, opening them this time, and discovered that one had been refilled with a saline solution. Clearly, Genene had used an entire bottle to paralyze children. When Kathleen discovered that another bottle of succinylcholine had gone missing, she fired Genene.

It was too late.

Families left her practice and her privileges were suspended. She became the target of lawsuits, and her husband divorced her to keep his assets from legal involvement. Chelsea McClellan's body was exhumed;

lab tests found that there was a presence of succinylcholine in her blood.

A grand jury was convened in January 1983, and it was found that 47 children had died in suspicious circumstances at Bexar Counter Medical Center Hospital. Genene had been present during all of their deaths.

Although Genene tried unsuccessfully to escape and made up stories of receiving death threats, she was arrested and the trial began. Kathleen Holland, now disgraced as a doctor, turned on her nurse and began to supply the court with everything they needed.

Genene was sentenced to 99 years in prison for the murder of 15-month-old Chelsea McClellan, later receiving a sentence to a concurrent term of 60 years for the damage she had done to Rolando Santos.

Justice was served, but the families still wept. To this day, Genene argues that she didn't kill anyone and only followed instructions provided by the doctors above her.

Genene was set to be released in 2018, but as of current circumstances involving an indictment on May 25, 2017, for the murder of Joshua Sawyer, she will now be prosecuted again and a fresh sentence issued.

It looks like our *Killer Nurse* is going to be behind bars for a long time...

Dr. Kathleen Holland — to some a culprit, to others a victim — continues to treat children in the Kerrville, Texas area. She is an esteemed doctor, and has since been forgiven for her involvement in Genene Jones' employment.

# Conclusion

*"The two most important days in your life are the day you are born and the day that you find out why."*

- Mark Twain

Life is a delicate, ephemeral experience that allows us a short moment in time to realize who and what we are. Many seek to do great deeds, others to do nothing of value at all. The people in this book are or were humans just like us; human beings that made their own decisions and had their own dreams.

Serial killers are usually not monsters; they are broken humans who have not tried hard enough to fight their demons and haven't received enough care from their family, friends, or community. We should seek to eliminate serial killers — not by killing them or throwing them behind bars forever, but by treating them before they can cause pain as we have read about in this book.

The world shall be a better place for it, and we will never have to hear of their kind again.

Ah, anyway. It's been an interesting journey. We hope you've liked it.

## THANKS FOR READING!

*Preview of*

# True Crime Stories

## 12 Terrifying True Crime Murder Cases

(List of Twelve Vol 1)

# Introduction

**W**hy is it that we are fascinated by stories and news coverage about murders? What is it about killers' morbid deeds that attract our interest? Some murders have become a permanent fixture in our popular culture. Books, movies, and even music have used particular murders as their subject matter. Perhaps our fascination with murderers arises as a vestige from our childhood. Perhaps we graduate from our childhood fascination with monsters to an adult fascination with murderers. Perhaps it is because murderers put into practice what we have all felt at times but could never conceive doing. After all, how many of us, in our most emotional moments, have felt like killing someone?

Between news coverage and popular culture, we have, intentionally or not, adopted beliefs about murders, many of which are inaccurate. Many of our assumptions about murders could lead us to a false sense of security.

We may wrongly believe there is a certain profile or set of qualities that murderers possess, that will help us intuitively tell whether or not the person next to us could take a human life.

Interviews with murderers have led to some surprising discoveries:

1.     Most murderers are not cold-blooded monsters that lack any sense of humanity. Most murderers are people who are suffering emotionally and have never received help.

2.     Murderers do not kill indiscriminately or without reason. Murderers kill due to their distorted thinking.

3.     Murderers are not born to kill; they almost have always experienced or witnessed extreme trauma when young.  Examples being physical abuse, sexual abuse, domestic violence, and drug abuse. The Adverse Childhood Experience Scale assesses a person's exposure to ten different traumatic events. Most of us would meet one of these criteria. Interviews with murderers have shown that most of them have experienced between nine and ten of these events.

In this book, you will read about twelve murderers. These individuals were selected because they are unfamiliar to many of us. While they may be less well-known than those murderers who have been highly publicized, their crimes are no less heinous. The murderers who will be covered in this book include:

• Marjorie Orbin, a former stripper who killed and dismembered her husband. To date, only his torso has been found.

• Christy Sheats, a mother who shot her two daughters at the dinner table to spite her husband.

• Luke Magnotta, a former male stripper and porn star who videotaped himself stabbing a man to death with an ice pick and then mailed his body parts to political offices and schools.

• Shari Tobyne, who dismembered her husband and distributed his body parts across three different counties.

• David Michael Barnett, the 20-year-old who stabbed both of his grandparents to death.

• Arunya Rouch, a petite woman who shot up the grocery store where she worked and murdered one of her co-workers.

• Brian Nichols, who went on a killing spree in a Georgia courtroom and was convicted on 50 charges.

- Valerie Pape, a wealthy Scottsdale Salon owner, who dismembered her husband. The media dubbed her case the "Trunk Murders."

- Robert Beaver, the 18-year-old who, with his brother, murdered their entire family.

- Amy Bishop, a university professor who shot her coworkers because she did not receive tenure.

- Bryan Uyesugi, a Xerox repairman who shot eight of his co-workers, killing seven of them.

- Antoinette Renee Frank, a police officer who, while on duty, committed three murders and armed robbery.

# ONE

---------------------------

# Marjorie Orbin

**"W**hat this seems to be is a revelation of your very darkest side, ma'am," said Judge Arthur Anderson, as he stared at Marjorie Orbin during her sentencing hearing. "When that dark side is unleashed, it's about as dark as it gets," he continued.

The judge spoke these words from his bench on September 8th, 2004, in a courtroom in Phoenix, Arizona. It was the start of fall in Arizona; a welcome reprieve from the blistering heat of the summer. It was not only the torrid heat that ended, however, but also a dark chapter of this desert community's crime annals.

# A Grisly Find

The residents of Phoenix enjoy a patchwork of preserved desert areas throughout the city. However, on October 23rd, 2004, the rugged beauty of these areas was eclipsed by a morbid find at the corner of Tatum and Dynamite Road, in North Phoenix. The Phoenix Police Department's 911 call center received a panicked call from an individual who was hiking in the area.

Police quickly arrived at the desert location and the hiker led them to a spot that was not far off from the residential streets that surrounded the reservation. When the officers reached the site, they instantly knew that this was not a routine call. Detective Dave Barnes, of the Missing Persons Unit, arrived on the scene minutes later. A putrid smell filled the air as Barnes walked toward a 50-gallon Rubber Maid container. "As we walked up you could smell the death in the air. Once you smell it, you know what it is for the rest of your life...it's the first time I had ever seen anything like that, where it's – just a piece of body," he would later say.

Barnes removed the lid and carefully opened the black trash bag contained within. Inside the trash bag was the bloody, dismembered torso of an adult male. Barnes would later tell a reporter, "All of the insides, all of the internal organs, intestines were missing…I thought, 'Who could do this to a human being? Cut off his arms, his legs, his head?'"

The grisly find was located less than two miles from the home of Marjorie Orbin, who lived in the 17000 block of North 55th Street. Butcher had a strong suspicion that he had just found the torso of her missing husband; Marjorie had filed a missing person report on September 22nd, 2004.

Jay Orbin was the successful owner of Jayhawk International, a dealership that specialized in Native American Art. He frequently traveled for business purposes and it was not unusual for him to be gone three weeks out of the month. It was through his business travels that Jay had first met Marjorie.

## The Stripper and the Salesman

Marjorie had been married seven times before meeting Jay at the age of 35. Marjorie was unable to conceive children and had lived a life with herself as the central focus. She entered each relationship looking for her Prince Charming, but it never happened. Her last relationship was with Michael J. Peter, a very successful businessman who had made millions of dollars creating upscale strip clubs around the world. Marjorie left Peter because she believed he was cheating on her. She moved to Las Vegas where she danced at a strip club. It was at this strip club in 1993 that she met Jay, who was traveling through Las Vegas. They had been dating for a while when Jay proposed to Marjorie, offering to pay for fertility treatments if she married him. Marjorie accepted Jay's proposal and they got married at the Little White Wedding Chapel in Las Vegas. Soon afterward, they moved to Phoenix, where Jay lived. Marjorie was able to conceive and gave birth to their son, Noah. The couple divorced in 1997 but continued to live together. Marjorie had problems with the IRS and did not want Jay's assets to be vulnerable.

## Jay's Disappearance

On September 8th, 2004, Jay was driving back to Phoenix from a business meeting when he got a call from his mother wishing him a happy birthday. That phone call was the last time anyone heard from Jay. When Jay's parents, brothers, and friends called his home, Marjorie told them that he had gone on a business trip and would not be returning until September 20th. During that time, those who cared about Jay could not reach him on his cell phone. His parents and friends expressed their concern to Marjorie; however, she said she did not know what was going on with him. Those who spoke to Marjorie about Jay stated that she expressed little concern for his welfare. Jay's intended return date passed and those who tried to reach him remained unsuccessful. When they inquired with Marjorie, she continued to remain aloof to their concerns. After continued pressure from friends and family, Marjorie notified the Phoenix Police on September 22nd.

## Suspicion is Raised

The Police Department assigned Detective Jan Butcher to the case. He interviewed Marjorie, who indicated that the last time she'd seen Jay was on August 28th, when he'd attended his son's birthday. Butcher began to be suspicious of Marjorie on September 28th, after he had left three voicemail messages for her before she called him back. "I asked her to provide me information on the license plate of the vehicle Jay was driving. She said she would call me back. She never did.

So that was a little bit odd," he later told a reporter. From that point on, Butcher's suspicions only continued to grow. Credit card and phone tower records indicated that Jay had arrived at his home in Phoenix on September 28th, which didn't match Marjorie's claim that she had last seen him on August 28th.

When detectives checked Jay's credit card records, they found that Marjorie was spending thousands of dollars, including the purchase of a $12,000 baby grand piano, while the business account had a withdrawal of $45,000. Within one day of being reporting Jay missing, she had liquidated a total of $100,000 from Jay's personal and business accounts.

A final cause for suspicion arose during a call that Detective Butcher made to Marjorie requesting that she take a polygraph test. Butcher heard Marjorie remark to someone in the background, "You know what? She wants me to take a polygraph tomorrow." A male voice replied, "You tell her to go f--- herself."

Butcher obtained a search warrant and went to Marjorie's home, accompanied by a SWAT team. The SWAT team forced their way in and encountered an adult male, Larry Weisberg. Larry was Marjorie's new boyfriend and the voice that had been heard in the background of the phone call. Weisberg was combative, resulting in police tasing him. Police searched the premises and found a large number of credit cards belonging to Jay, plus his business checkbook; items that he always kept with him when traveling. Though police did not make any arrests, their surveillance of Marjorie deepened. It was shortly after Marjorie's home was searched that police found Jay's torso in the Rubbermaid container in the desert.

DNA evidence confirmed the torso belonged to Jay Orbin. The Maricopa County Medical Examiner's Office inspected the torso and concluded Jay had been shot and his body frozen. At some point, the body had been defrosted, and a jigsaw was used to dismember and decapitate it. When searching Jay's business, police found a packet of jigsaw blades, with some of the blades missing. The Medical Examiner's Office determined the blades from the business matched the cut marks on the torso, where the limbs and vertebrae were severed.

Detectives traced the UPC code on the Rubbermaid container back to a Lowes Home Improvement store in Scottsdale. The detectives scored big when they viewed video from the store's surveillance cameras and saw Marjorie purchasing the Rubber Maid container, the trash bag, and black tape. Police detained Marjorie when they caught her forging Jay's signature while making a purchase at a Circuit City store.

Jay's remaining body parts were never found, nor the gun that was used to shoot Jay. Marjorie and her boyfriend, Larry Weisberg, were arrested on December 6th, 2004. Weisberg was offered immunity if he agreed to testify against Marjorie, who was sentenced to life in prison on October 1st, 2009.

# TWO

------------------------------

## Christy Sheats

Located just northeast of Houston, the city of Katy has a population of 16,158, according to 2015 statistics. On June 24th, 2016, a 911 dispatcher received a chilling call. At first, the dispatcher did not hear a single voice talking to her, as was the norm for most calls. Rather, she could hear several voices in the background. Then she heard the sound of a female crying and the words, "Please. Forgive me. Please. Don't shoot." This was followed by a male voice that begged, "Please. Don't point that gun at her." A gunshot sounded and the female voice yelled to the dispatcher, "I'm shot." The dispatcher answered, "Hello? What's the address?" There was no response. The phone went dead.

# Fatal Meeting

That phone call originated from the home of Jason and Christy Sheats. Christy, age 42, was born in Decatur, Alabama, as was Jason. They were childhood sweethearts who had eventually moved to Katy, Texas, where they raised their two daughters; 17-year-old Madison and 22-year-old Taylor. Jason worked for Oxy, a Houston-based oil company, as an IT consultant. In recent years, the Sheats had experienced marital problems and Jason was planning to divorce Christy. On the day of that fateful phone call, it was Jason's 45th birthday and Christy had called a family meeting around 5:00 p.m. Jason and their daughters expected the meeting to be about the looming divorce.

The family gathered around the dining table. Within seconds, the unimaginable occurred. Christy pulled out a .38-caliber revolver that she had been hiding under the table. She pointed it at Taylor and shot her in the back as she tried to run away from the table. Christy then turned to Madison and shot her in the neck. Jason ran and took refuge behind the living room couch, before fleeing with his daughters out the front door. However, the daughters only made it to the street before both of them collapsed. Christy started running toward Taylor, who was lying on the street, while a neighbor offered Jason shelter in her home. The police, who arrived in time to witness this chaos, used trees and parked cars as shields. They saw Christy kneeling over Taylor's body, ready to shoot her a second time. Police ordered her to drop the gun. When she refused, they shot her.

A medical helicopter took Taylor to a local hospital where she died on arrival. Madison and Christy's lifeless bodies lay on the street in front of their home. The gun that Christy used was a gift from her grandfather, to whom she was extremely close.

## Downward Spiral

Christy was deeply impacted when her grandfather died in 2012. Compounding her grief was the fact that her grandmother died two months later. Jason would later tell detectives that his wife suffered from depression during this time and became a heavy drinker. She had been admitted to a private mental health hospital for suicide attempts three times in the last four years. Jason stated that Christy took a variety of prescription medications and was seeing a therapist. A neighbor informed the police the couple had separated but then had recently reconciled. Before the shooting, Christy had no history of acting violently toward others.

Christy had stopped working after the death of her grandfather. Previously, she had worked as a hair stylist, as an executive assistant to the vice-president of a transportation company, and as a receptionist at Clean Canvas Tattoo Removal. This was a part-time position that she had held from January 2015 to May 2015, when she was fired. The owner, John Hollis, had originally thought that Christy was the perfect fit for the job. In an interview with People, he stated, "She was very pleasant when she wanted to be. That was in front of customers." He went on, "The times when she wasn't pleasant were times were when I assumed that whatever was going on at home was getting to her."

Hollis also indicated that Christy had spent some time living in an apartment, away from the rest of the family. She would flip flop in her explanations about this to Hollis, sometimes saying that she was separated from her husband and other times stating that she was going to divorce him. "It was erratic; it was highs-and-lows," Hollis continued. "I wouldn't say it was deterioration; I would say it was peaks and valleys."

## Mixed Messages

The interviews conducted by the media with those who knew her, and through the Sheats' active use of social media provide a different perspective on Christy. A friend, Catherine Knowles, commented to People Magazine, "She loves her daughters. I have no idea what could possibly make a mother who loves her daughters as much as she did – what could cause a person to snap? The part of Christy that I knew was a very kind, loving mother." Knowles continued, "Within 20 seconds of meeting her, we were talking about her being a mom. That was her mission in life, that was her everything – her two daughters."

On Daughter's Day in September of the year prior to the shooting, Christy posted the following message to her Facebook account:

"Happy Daughter's Day to my two amazing, sweet, kind, beautiful, intelligent girls," she wrote. "I love and treasure you both more than you could ever possibly know."

Three years before the shooting, Taylor posted the following message to her Facebook account, honoring her mother on Mother's Day:

"Mom, you are so selfless, as you always put our whole family before yourself and never ask for anything in return," the post read. "You're so kind and loving, as you always remind us of just how much you care and how proud you are of everything we do. You're so intelligent and fun to be around because I feel like I can talk to you for forever now about anything."

The post concluded: "You're one of the strongest people I know, if not the strongest, and you have had to overcome so much in your life, but you still manage to love us and put your everything into being a mom. You're so encouraging, as you always push us to do our absolute best, even when we can't muster up the strength to do it ourselves. You're such a blessing to have as a mother and friend, and I truly appreciate you and all that you do. Happy Mother's Day to my amazing mommy and I love you."

Two years before the shooting, Christy posted on her Facebook page: "I am truly a Southern gal. I was born in Alabama, but have been living here in Texas for 15 years. I have two amazing daughters I simply adore... They are my everything! I thank God for every breath he allows me to take!!"

When a reporter for the Houston Chronicle interviewed one of Christy's neighbors, Austin Enke, he stated, "They were always cheerful and never depressed. You never heard anything bad about them." While another neighbor told a local news station, "The mother was nice. You wouldn't expect it if they told you this is what was going to happen. I don't think anybody, at least a sane person, would do that."

Neighbor Catherine Knowles told KTRK-TV, "This is not the Christy that I know. It's just not. I thought it was the wrong person. It had to be…When you meet her, you know she's a mom within the first minute. I couldn't imagine anything in her life that could've made her snap. Your own children, I don't know what could possibly go through someone's head."

In one Facebook post, Christy referred to herself as being Baptist, as well as conservative and strong supporter of the second amendment; which provides the right for gun ownership. In one Facebook post, she wrote, "It would be horribly tragic if my ability to protect myself or my family were to be taken away, but that's exactly what Democrats are determined to do by banning semi-automatic handguns."

## The Last Argument

On the day of the killing, Christy and Jason had gotten into an argument over Taylor, who had a fiancée, Juan Sebastian Lugo. Taylor and Lugo started seeing each other in 2011 and he had given her a promise ring in 2013.

Christy wanted to ground Taylor and prohibit her from seeing Lugo. Jason argued that he was agreeable to grounding Taylor, but said they could not disallow her from seeing Lugo. Others knew Jason to be a doting father to his daughters. The reason for Taylor's punishment was not known, but later that morning, Jason told Christy, "This would be the last birthday that you are going to ruin."

After the shooting, Madison Davey, a friend of the Sheats family, spoke to a local news reporter and related a conversation that he'd had with Jason on the morning of the shooting. According to Davey, Jason said he had told Christy on the day of the shooting, "Just shoot yourself. Make it easy on all of us, just shoot yourself." He said Christy replied back to him, "No, that's not what this is about, this is about punishing you.'" Davey then told the reporter, "I always knew something would happen, but I never thought she would do this. Christy was toxic for the family. She was mentally unstable...He [Jason] would do anything to protect them and he tried to, but Christy was out to kill that day."

Police believe that Christy shot their daughters because that would cause the greatest pain for Jason, adding that Christy could have easily just killed Jason if she wanted. Knowing how much Jason loved his girls, killing them and letting him live would create the greatest suffering for him.

# THREE

------------------------------

# Luke Magnotta

Luke Magnotta, whose birth name was Eric Clinton Kirk Newman, was born July 24th, 1982, in Scarborough, Canada. Newman's troubled past, including a track record of attention-seeking, would culminate in him becoming the subject of the largest manhunt in the history of Montreal, which would eventually extend internationally.

**The Early Years**

Anna Yourk and Donald Newman, Luke's parents, separated when he was very young. Luke was the oldest of three children. He and his two younger sisters were sent to live with their grandparents. Newman's high school teachers and classmates remembered him as self-obsessed about his looks. Newman dropped out of high school and began work as a stripper at a Toronto nightclub at the age of 19. He also worked as an escort and appeared in pornographic videos, both gay and straight.

Newman perpetrated his first crime in his early twenties. He had won the trust of a woman with a mental handicap and persuaded her to apply for credit cards. Newman committed fraud by making charges on the cards that totaled $10,000. He also was suspected of sexually assaulting the woman.

The sexual assault charges were dropped due to medical reports that indicated Newman had a significant psychiatric issue. Instead, Newman was found guilty on four counts of fraud and received probation and community service. Looking back at the decision to drop the charges, Newman's defense attorney stated that this had changed the course of Newman's life and the impact was "immeasurable, with huge ramifications for our society eventually."

Newman then began dating a transgender woman who would later tell investigators that Newman wanted to be famous and would beg her to take pictures of him. She described his apartment as "looking like a shrine dedicated to himself." Their relationship lasted several months before they broke up. Shortly afterward, Newman changed his name to Luka Rocco Magnotta.

## Starving for Attention

At age the age of 25, Magnotta attended auditions for reality television shows in his continued effort to become famous. During an audition for one of the shows, he told the judges, "Some people say I am devastatingly good-looking." One of the shows he auditioned for was Plastic Makes Perfect; which features contestants who have had plastic surgery. He told the judges, during his audition, "I've had my nose done. I've had two hair transplants...and I'm planning on having muscle implants in my pecs and my arms." Magnotta failed to make the cut for any of the shows for which he auditioned.

When his efforts to get on television failed, Magnotta became heavily involved with social media, opening multiple accounts on Facebook and other platforms. He used accounts that were set-up under aliases to spread rumors about himself and then used accounts that were established under his real name to defend himself. His online efforts to promote himself took a disturbing turn in 2010 when he posted a video link to his Facebook page titled, '3 Guys 1 Hammer.'

The video showed a man being brutally beaten and killed. Magnotta did not have any involvement in the murder, but personalized the posting with the tag, "Luka is unable to live unless there is chaos in his life, it makes him feel as though he matters."

Just before Christmas that year, he posted a second video called, '1 Guy-2 Kittens.' The video showed an unidentified man (his face was not visible) using a vacuum cleaner to suck the air out of a plastic bag that contained two kittens.

Outrage over the kitten video led to the formation of Facebook groups whose mission was to locate Magnotta and bring him to justice. The groups collaborated with law enforcement, but their efforts yielded minimal results during their first year of investigations. Magnotta's online activity was rampant in early 2012, as he posted countless blogs about necrophilia and sedatives. Toward midyear, an online promotion for a yet-to-be-released video titled, '1 Lunatic 1 Ice Pick' surfaced. The animal rights groups who were looking for

Magnotta believed he was responsible for this video as well.

## Reaching the Tipping Point

On May 25th, just a few days after the promotional video had been released, the full-length video of '1 Lunatic 1 Ice Pick' appeared online. The eleven-minute video opened with a shot of a naked male tied to a bed frame. The person operating the video camera, who is not visible to the viewer, violently attacks the restrained man by repeatedly stabbing him, first with an ice pick and then with a kitchen knife. Toward the end, the assailant removes a piece of flesh from his victim and feeds it to a dog.

On May 29th, the receptionist on the 12th floor of the Conservative Party's headquarters received a package. She started to open it but became suspicious when she noticed bloodstains and detected a putrid smell. Staffers called the Ottawa Police Department; who responded with a Hazmat crew. When they opened the package, they found a human foot.

Two elementary schools; St. George School and False Creek Elementary School, both received similar packages on June 5th. The St. George package contained a right foot, while the package sent to False Creek contained a right hand. The packages were sent from Montreal, where Magnotta was currently living.

Around the same time, other packages showed up containing body parts. A package containing a left hand was located at the processing facility of the Canadian Post Office; the package was addressed to Canada's Liberal Party. On May 25th, a janitor for an apartment building in Montreal noticed a suitcase in the building's alley. Inside it, he found a badly decomposed torso.

## The Investigation

Police interviewed residents in the area where the torso was found, looking for possible clues. While conducting their interviews, they learned that Magnotta had an apartment nearby. Police went to his apartment, but the apartment manager informed them that Magnotta had recently moved. When the manager let the police into the now-vacated apartment, they found bloodstains on a mattress and table that Magnotta had left behind. They also found bloodstains in the bathtub. Police discovered the following message written in red ink on the inside of a cupboard door, "If you don't like the reflection. Don't look in the mirror. I don't care." They then viewed the video from the apartment's security camera. The video showed an individual resembling Magnotta carrying out a large number of garbage bags.

On May 30th, 2012, detectives got a hit on the identification of the body parts; they belonged to Lin Jun, a Chinese national who was attending Concordia University in Montreal. On July 1st, Jun's decapitated head was found at Angrignom Park in Montreal. A visitor to the park found the head at the edge of the lake.

The Montreal Police issued an arrest warrant for Magnotta, which was later upgraded to an arrest warrant applicable throughout Canada. Magnotta faced charges including first-degree murder, committing an indignity to a dead body, the publishing of obscene material, mailing obscene, indecent, immoral, or scurrilous material, and criminally harassing the Canadian Prime Minister and several members of parliament.

A Red Notice was issued by Interpol on May 31st, 2012, and Magnotta's photograph was posted on the Interpol website. The Red Notice gave any Interpol member state permission to arrest Magnotta pending extradition back to Canada.

Unbeknownst to Montreal authorities, Magnotta had flown to Paris on May 25th, using his own passport. After the Interpol Red Notice was issued, Paris officials were able to track his movement by following his cell phone signal. They traced him to a hotel in the city of Bagnolet; however, he had left by the time police arrived. Authorities found pornographic magazines in his hotel room.

From Paris, Magnotta flew to Berlin, Germany. On June 4th Berlin police located Magnotta in an internet café in Neukolln, a district of Berlin, where he was reading the latest news about himself. On June 5th Magnotta appeared in a Berlin court. He was extradited back to Canada and a preliminary hearing was held in a high-security Montreal courtroom on March 11th, 2013.

## On Trial

Magnotta elected to have a trial by jury and pleaded not guilty. He did not deny that he had done everything that he was charged with but claimed diminished responsibility due to mental disorders. The prosecutor argued that Jun Lin's murder was organized and premeditated, saying that Magnotta was "purposeful, mindful, ultra-organized and ultimately responsible for his actions."

Magnotta's attorney offered evidence that his client had been diagnosed with paranoid schizophrenia when he was a teenager. A psychiatrist for the defense, Dr. Joel Watts, testified that Magnotta showed symptoms of borderline personality disorder, histrionic personality disorder, and episodic schizophrenia. The prosecutor argued the symptoms described by the defense expert were the result of Magnotta's drug use as a teenager.

Magnotta did not testify during the 12-week trial. On December 15th, 2014, the jury started deliberating, and by December 23rd, they found Magnotta guilty on all charges. He received a mandatory life sentence, plus an additional 19 years for related charges. Though Magnotta filed an appeal, claiming judicial error during jury instructions, he later withdrew it.

There are many people in society who feel isolated from others and hungry for attention. When we act indifferently towards others, some of these people will raise the stakes until they get noticed. Magnotta was one such individual.

# FOUR

------------------------

# Shari Tobyne

$\mathbf{W}$hile Arizona is known for its extreme heat, the seasons of fall and winter bring temperatures that are much more pleasant. Outdoor enthusiasts take full advantage of the weather and the natural beauty of the Copper State at that time of year. Unfortunately, such pleasures were not awaiting a group of outdoor adventurers in December 2010.

## The Disbursement of Body Parts

While hiking in Pinal County, some individuals came across a gruesome discovery. They found human remains off the U.S. 60 Highway, just south of Florence

Junction. The remains were sent to the Pinal County Medical Examiner's Office in Tucson.

On December 23rd, hikers in La Paz County found body parts off Interstate 10, near mile marker 53, just 50 miles from the California border. Again, the remains were sent to the Pima County Medical Examiner's Office.

On December 26th, a driver on the Beeline Highway spotted partial human remains off the side of the road near the Sugarloaf off ramp. Those remains were turned over to the Maricopa County Medical Examiner's Office.

## A Family's Concern

Five months earlier, the adult children of 57-year-old-Dwight Tobyne contacted the Scottsdale Police Department. They were concerned about their father's welfare, as they had lost contact with him. He had not shown up for Christmas or the birth of his grandchild. Their mother, Shari Tobyne, had told her children their father had gone to Mexico and would be returning in late November.

Detectives visited Shari Tobyne at her condominium in the 8000 block of East Mountain View Road. During their interview, detectives became suspicious of Shari, as she was unable to answer their questions directly. As a result, they put her under surveillance. They saw her placing a large trash bag in the dumpster behind a store in Chandler, Arizona. When the trash bag was recovered, police found a gun and pieces of clothing inside. Later, they observed Tobyne visiting a self-serve car wash, where she spray cleaned the trunk of her car. Tobyne was arrested and brought to the Scottsdale Police Department for further questioning. At the time, the Scottsdale Police were not aware the Arizona Department of Public Safety crime lab had determined that the human remains found in the three different countries all belong to the same individual.

## Eliminating Hubby

During the August 14th interview, Tobyne told detectives she had bought the gun with the intention of using it to kill herself. She divulged that her husband, Dwight, had advised her he was leaving her and moving back to Oklahoma, after 35 years of marriage. Tobyne described Dwight's death as follows: she walked into their bedroom with the gun pointed at her head, but when Dwight jumped up from bed to grab it from her, the gun accidentally went off, killing him.

Tobyne explained she feared no one would believe it was an accident, so she wrapped up Dwight's body in a tarp, placed him in her car, and dumped his body in the Tonto Forest, along the Bush Highway. She also stated she replaced the master bedroom carpet due to the blood spatter. When Tobyne took investigators to the location where she claimed to have dumped the body, they found no trace of human remains.

As detectives continued their investigation, they found additional evidence that contradicted the statements

Tobyne made during the first interview. For example, they uncovered the story Tobyne told her children about their father leaving her and going to Mexico in late November. Dwight and Shari's cell phone records showed both cell phones had been in the Phoenix area between November 24th and December 25th. Police also learned Tobyne had bought a handgun in early November and had taken shooting lessons. Further, Dwight Tobyne's truck had been found parked at a Phoenix apartment complex, near 30th Street and Shea Avenue. The doors were locked, the keys were in the ignition, and the battery was dead.

Detectives talked to the owner of the Tobyne's condominium on Mountain View, from whom the Tobyne's had been renting. The owner confirmed that Shari Tobyne had replaced the bedroom carpet and the garage smelt strongly of bleach.

During their second interview with Tobyne, detectives confronted her with the new evidence. She confessed to killing her husband because he was leaving her. She had shot him on November 24, 2009, the day before he had planned to leave for Oklahoma. No one knew he was dead because she had used his phone and email account to send messages to friends and family to avoid suspicion.

## Charges and Prosecution

The charges against Tobyne for first-degree murder would be challenging to prove because authorities still did not have a body. According to the district attorney in the Tobyne case, the pursuit of a murder charge without a body had been achieved successfully before, but such cases were rare. He could remember only two or three instances in Phoenix where there was a prosecution without a body within the last 25 years.

On October 7th, 2010, detectives finally received news about human remains found in the three counties all had come from the same individual. Detectives were able to get a DNA sample from Dwight Tobyne's father, who lived in Kansas. His DNA sample was a close enough match to determine the human remains belonged to Dwight Tobyne.

On May 19th, 2013, Tobyne was sentenced to life in prison. She received an additional 31 years for related charges.

# FIVE

------------------------------

## David Michael Barnett

**"I** just snapped." These were David Barnett's chilling words to the reporter who was interviewing him. Barnett's story is one of heinous violence and a challenge to the death penalty. Barnett was born May 18th, 1976, in Glendale, Missouri. He grew up in a severely dysfunctional home. His father was a violent alcoholic and his mother made frequent attempts to abandon David. After David was born, his mother tried to leave the hospital without him and she later tried to leave him with a drug-addicted sex worker.

By the age of five-years-old, Barnett had been removed from his parent's home and placed in a series of foster homes. His grandparents eventually adopted him. By eight years old, Barnett was contemplating suicide. He survived an overdose on prescription drugs when he was in his late teens.

## Deadly Sunday

Barnett's fateful day was Sunday, February 4th, 1996, at 8:00 a.m. His grandparents were attending a service at the Kirkwood Baptist Church. Barnett, who was aged twenty at the time, was spending time more and more time living with his friends, as he was not getting along with his grandparents. His grandparents were getting frustrated with him because of his delinquent behavior.

That terrible morning, Barnett walked back from his friends' house to his grandparents' home. When he arrived, he entered the house through the bedroom window. He then lay down on the living room couch and fell asleep while watching television. His grandparents returned from church around 1:00 p.m. They were upset to find he had entered the home. An argument ensued and Barnett shoved his grandmother, causing her to fall to the floor. She lay there helplessly as her grandson violently shoved her husband. With both his grandparents on the floor, David made his way into the kitchen, grabbed a knife that was on the kitchen table.

He returned to the living room and stood over his dazed and confused grandparents. They could not believe what was happening to them. Barnett kicked his grandfather in the head as he struggled to get up. He stabbed his grandfather savagely a total of ten times in the head and hands. His grandfather's blood drained out of his dying body and covered the living room rug. When he was sure his grandfather was dead, Barnett returned to the kitchen to get another knife. Returning to the living room, he headed for his grandmother. With rage still coursing through his veins, he repeatedly stabbed her around the neck. The anger that he felt for his grandmother remained, despite the fact she lay dying. He returned to the kitchen yet again and returned with two new knives. He continued to stab her in the neck and face. By the time he was done, Barnett's grandmother had 12 stab wounds to her neck.

With his grandparents dead on the living floor, Barnett hid the knives, placing one between the mattresses of his grandparent's bed. He washed the blood off his hands in the bathroom and then headed for the garage. Barnett had previously told his friends how much he wanted his grandfather's car, a 1995 Dodge Intrepid. He knew where his grandfather kept the keys, which he now obtained. He also took $120 from his grandmother's purse before driving away in the Intrepid.

## Surrender

Police discovered the dead bodies of Barnett's grandparents by the next morning and commenced a search of the area. They found the stolen Intrepid in a nearby residential neighborhood. As they were inspecting the car, Barnett approached them and confessed to the murders.

The jury in Barnett's trial found him guilty and he was convicted of two counts of first-degree murder. Prosecutors sought the death penalty during the sentencing phase, but Barnett's attorney asked for leniency, stating the Barnett suffered from post-traumatic stress, bipolar disorder, and depression. He also pointed to Barnett's childhood, which he described as "unstable." The jury deliberated for two days and decided on the death penalty.

Barnett appealed the death penalty decision, stating his attorney had failed to present information about the abuse and neglect he had experienced during his childhood. His appeal was denied; however, Judge E. Richard Webber ruled in Barnett's favor, stating that during the trial there was no mention of Barnett's violent and alcoholic father, that Barnett had been sexually abused, nor any mention that his mother had made numerous attempts to abandon him. In Webber's words "at least one juror would have determined the balance of aggravating and mitigating circumstances did not warrant death in Mr. Barnett's case." Webber made the determination the attorney general could appeal the case if they wanted to pursue the death penalty, or Barnett would be sentenced to life in prison without parole. The latter eventually became Barnett's sentence.

Every child is like a sponge; they absorb the emotions given off by those around them. Children retain the energy from these emotions and it becomes part of them. Barnett's story is an example of how family violence and neglect can destroy lives.

# SIX

--------------------------

## Arunya Rouch

**A**runya Rouch sat stoically next to her defense attorney in a St. Petersburg, Florida courtroom. She didn't show any hint of reaction or emotion as trial proceedings came to a close, nor as friends and family members tearfully addressed her with their victim impact statements, nor when the jury of nine women and three men found her guilty of murder. Nor did she react when the judge gave her a life sentence. It took the jury seven hours of deliberation to reach their verdict; a surprise to most who had predicted the deliberations would be over much sooner.

# Going back to the Beginning

Arunya Rouch was born in Thailand, where she lived in poverty. Looking for a better life, she moved to the United States and gained citizenship. Her husband, Tom Rouch and Arunya, worked for Tarpon Springs Publix; an employee-owned grocery store chain. Rouch was a trainer for the company and in charge of opening seafood departments in new stores. On March 30th, 2010, Arunya Rouch, 41, was fired from Tarpon Springs Publix for making threats to a coworker who had planned to report Rouch for infringing company policy. Tarpon Springs Publix had a policy against working without clocking in first. The co-worker who planned to report Rouch was Gregory Janowski.

# Grocery Store Shooting

Rouch left work upset with Janowski and other co-workers, whom she felt had disrespected her. At home, she grabbed a 9mm semiautomatic weapon and returned to work.

Upon arriving back at Tarpon Springs Publix, she saw Janowski sitting in his car in the parking lot. Rouch approached the parked car, took aim, and fatally shot him.

Janowski slumped forward; his blood dripped onto the car seat and floor, forming a pool. Rouch then ran toward Tarpon Springs Publix. She was going to shoot her manager and the co-workers who had disgraced her.

Entering the building, she made her way toward her manager's office. The sight of a gun-toting Rouch instantly generated panic in the crowed store. Chaos broke out as shoppers screamed, dropped their groceries, and fled for their lives. People were trampling over each other as they rushed to the door.

A witness to the parking lot shooting had called 911. As the Tarpon Springs Police Department was just a block away from Tarpon Springs Publix, two officers arrived as Rouch entered the store. They rushed in the store and Rouch fired at them; a bullet grazed one of the officers. Rouch was able to get a few more shots off before one of the officers was able to shoot Rouch, wounding her. Police took Rouch to Bayfront Medical Center for treatment.

## Motives and Sentencing

According to the FBI, Rouch was a rare case; as women commit only 5% of workplace homicides. Experts in workplace violence say that part of the reason for this low number is that women, unlike men, tend not to act violently in the workplace unless all other options fail. Further, when they do act violently, it is usually the results of long-term frustration, while men commit workplace violence to show they are in charge.

Rouch was married but did not have children and she was a perfectionist at work. This rubbed many of her co-workers the wrong way. Those who knew her stated she loved her job and would often prepare food at home for her co-workers. Her husband, Tom Rouch, believed that she killed out of the sense she had disgraced her family by losing her job.

During Rouch's trial, her husband testified she had experienced chronic bullying by some of her co-workers and that management of Tarpon Springs Publix hadn't done anything to stop this. In his emotional testimony, Tom Rouch stated that his wife had been treated "like an animal" at work. He further stated that Janowski was the main culprit in the bullying and that in one incident, Janowski and other coworkers had locked Arunya in a seafood freezer. Rouch had no history of mental illness and was found guilty of one count of first-degree murder, two counts of attempted first-degree murder, and two counts of aggravated assault.

Those who harass others do so because it gives them a sense of power. They pick a victim who they feel is vulnerable; an easy target. When a target, like Arunya, reaches their breaking point, they may strike back in unexpectedly deadly ways.

Want more? Guess what? You can read the rest for free

on Amazon Kindle by visiting:

http://amzn.to/2zkQstf

*No sign up required. It is 100% free!*

# Free Book

Dark fantasies are something that exists in all our minds. Once unleashed into the real world, the transformation begins for what once to be considered normal into a cruel and terrifying murder.

**Turn The Page To Receive**

# Dark Fantasies Turn Reality

Sign up for the Ryan's VIP mailing list today to receive your free copy of the latest anthology of Serial Killer facts and trivia.

By being part of the mailing list you will be eligible for exclusive promotions, updates about new releases, as well as giveaways!!!

*Sign up here:* www.ryanbeckerwrites.com

# About the Author

Ryan Becker aims to write all the stories he has read and watched and letting himself be taken into the world of true mysteries and psychological murder crime stories. He also wants to share his experience of his younger days with the readers on how he immersed himself with the dark reality of the world. He loves to tell a true story that will make you solve a puzzle on your mind. He is now living with his wife and two sons. Ideally, Ryan wants to leave a mark on the reader with his dark true crime stories.

Follow Ryan:

Author Website: www.ryanbeckerwrites.com

Facebook: @ryanbeckerwrites

Twitter: @ryanbeckerwrites